Brenda Harty

Brenda Harty

LEARNING LANGUAGE AND LOVING IT

A Guide to
Promoting Children's
Social and Language Development
in Early Childhood Settings

Elaine Weitzman

A Hanen Centre Publication

Learning Language and Loving It
by Elaine Weitzman

A HANEN CENTRE PUBLICATION
Copyright 1992

Copies of this book may be ordered from the publisher: **THE HANEN CENTRE,**
252 Bloor Street West, Room 390,
Toronto, Ontario
M5S 1V5
(416) 921-1073
Fax (416) 921-1225

National Library of Canada
ISBN 0-921145-03-9

Parts of this book were adapted from "It Takes Two to Talk", a Hanen Parent Guidebook by Ayala Manolson (1985)

Illustrations: Ruth Ohi

Graphic design: Jerry Newton

Cover concept: Kevin Weitzman

"Learning Language and Loving It" is a publication of the Hanen Centre and was supported by funding from the Federal Department of Health and Welfare Canada through the Child Care Initiatives Fund. All views expressed herein are those of the author and do not necessarily reflect the views of the Department of Health and Welfare Canada.

Printed in Canada
by The Beacon Herald Fine Printing Division

LEARNING LANGUAGE AND LOVING IT

Elaine Weitzman

Table of Contents

Acknowledgements

Throughout the course of this project, I have enjoyed the enthusiastic support of many people who interrupted their busy schedules to contribute to the creation of this book.

Special thanks are due to Ayala Manolson, founder of the Hanen Language Program, for her perseverance in getting this project under way and for her unfailing interest, encouragement and support.

This book was made possible by funding from the Federal Department of Health and Welfare Canada through the Child Care Initiatives Fund, and I am grateful to Dawn Hachey, Regional Consultant, Health and Welfare Canada, whose belief in this project made it a reality.

Many colleagues and friends have helped me in a number of ways. I want to make special mention of my colleague, Fern Sussman, who has contributed many creative ideas to the Hanen Language Program for Early Childhood Educators and who has been so supportive over the years. Luigi Girolametto, fellow Speech-language Pathologist and Assistant Professor at University of Toronto's Department of Speech Pathology also helped by providing me with valuable comments on many of the chapters.

This book was enriched by the input of many Early Childhood Educators: Elaine Everett was of enormous assistance in converting theory into practice, and Shanley Pierce and Joan Arruda provided me with a great deal of insight into the field of child care. I must also thank the teachers at Air-O-Down and Start Right Child Care Centres (both in Toronto) who pilot-tested the first draft and gave me valuable feedback. There are many other teachers, too numerous to mention, whose creative ideas found their way into the program and onto the pages of this book.

I consider myself extremely fortunate to have had Jerry Newton as graphic designer; his talent and his ability to stay calm under pressure are both extraordinary. Thanks to Ruth Ohi for her wonderful illustrations and to Hugh Oliver for his excellent copy editing and for his patience in trying to show me how to use commas.

The Hanen office staff, Adele Ritchie, Tom Khan and Katie D'Alessandro have all been exceptionally helpful in so many aspects, and it has been a pleasure to work with them.

My family has been with me all the way. My parents-in-law, Dora and Raphie Weitzman, and my sister-in-law Sheila were always willing to assist in any way they could. My sisters, Margaret and Adele, gave me much moral support and my parents, Annette and Mick Schneider, who gave me such a strong foundation in literacy, have always been supportive and encouraging, despite the thousands of miles that separate us.

I have no adequate words for my husband Irvine, who helped me in more ways than I could ever describe. My children, Joanne and Kevin, also kept me going with their love, patience (most of the time) and offers of help. I can finally answer their question "What chapter are you on?" to their satisfaction.

A note on the use of "he" and "she"

Use of "he" and "she" is alternated in the chapters of this book, except for Chapter 2, where it alternates by section. For simplicity's sake, the teacher in this book is almost always referred to as "she". However, in recognition of the male teachers in the field of Early Childhood Education, the reader will notice that some of the illustrations and examples are of male teachers.

Foreword

A director of a child care centre in North York, Toronto, recently said:

> *"It is our responsibility to give each child the best experiences, knowledge and growth in all areas of development in order to put that child into a success mode for the rest of his life."*

A major part of this awesome responsibility involves promoting children's language development. But how do you do this when you work with large groups of children, including children with language delays? And how can you help those children who seem to be at-risk or those who are able to communicate, but seldom do? And then there are the children who speak little or no English — what about them? And those children who seem to be developing normally need attention too!

This guidebook is designed to help Early Childhood Educators promote the language learning of **all children**, but particularly the language learning of those who don't communicate as well as their peers. The information in this book is drawn from the Hanen Language Program for Early Childhood Educators, which provides on-site training in language facilitation to teachers who work in child care centres. This program, adapted from the Hanen Language Program for parents of language-delayed children, is based on the principle that children learn language as they interact with their caregivers and later, with their peers. The program aims to help teachers increase children's opportunities for interaction and language learning during everyday activities, routines and conversations.

The language facilitation techniques and strategies that are outlined in this book are consistent with the current child-centred approach to early childhood education. Many of them will be familiar to you. By making these strategies a natural part of your interactions with children, you can provide every child with an environment that fosters his or her social, emotional and intellectual development — an environment that promotes communication and language learning in an atmosphere of caring and sharing.

Elaine Weitzman

P A R T   1

TAKE A CLOSER LOOK AT COMMUNICATION

No matter how effortless learning to communicate may seem to be for many children, there are two conditions that must be fulfilled in order for communication to develop:

Interaction

Language learning takes place within the everyday interactions children have with their caregivers and, in time, with their peers. Ideally, these interactions should be fun and should occur often. And the child should participate actively in them because that's the only way he can learn to become a communicator.

Information

During interactions, children need their conversation partners to provide them with information that relates to the topic of the conversation. The information must be relevant and appropriate to the child's language level so he can use it to build upon what he already knows.

PART 1 of this book is about taking a closer look at communication so that you become aware of each child's need for both interaction and information.

In Chapter 1, we take "An Inside Look at Interactions in Child Care" and examine children's interactions with both teachers and peers. We see how teachers and children affect one another's interactive behaviour and how peer interactions change over time. And we see what happens to children who can't or don't participate fully in those critical everyday interactions.

In Chapter 2, "The Stages of Language Development: Talking Takes Time", we look at the stages of communication and language development so that you know what to expect from children at different ages and stages. As you read Parts 2, 3 and 4 of this book, your knowledge of the stages of language development will help you apply the information to the children with whom you work.

So read on. In taking a closer look at communication, you are taking an important first step in helping children become more accomplished communicators.

CHAPTER 1

An Inside Look at Interactions In Child Care

A. Teachers' Interactions with Children: Building Relationships that Build Communication

A new child comes
to the centre

André, aged 19 months, is new to Happy Days Child Care Centre. On this, his first day, his mother is about to leave and he knows it! He begins to kick and scream. Maria, his teacher, picks him up and tries to comfort him (and gets kicked in the process!).

What should Maria do next? What is the best way to handle a child who is new to the centre, very frightened and unsure of his surroundings?

It's worth thinking about, because what Maria does next will make an enormous difference to André — to how he feels about child care, to how he feels about himself and to how he will communicate with others.

She could comfort him for a while and, when he quietens down, leave him alone to see what he will do.

Or she could try to involve him in an activity with a group of children.

Or she could spend some time playing with him, so he can begin to develop a relationship with her.

Maria decides on the play and she takes André over to the sand table. After a while, he calms down and starts to dump sand. "Oh," says Maria, "You're dumping the sand!" She follows suit and then stops to watch him. He points to her pail as if to tell her "Do it again!" She does, saying "My turn to dump the sand? OK!" This turns into a dumping game, with Maria and André taking turns shovelling and dumping sand, smiling at each other a lot and Maria making comments as they play.

André's tears are gone and he seems quite content to play at the sand table. Even when Maria leaves him to attend to some other children, he continues to play.

Over the next few days Maria and André play the dumping game again. As he becomes more comfortable in his new surroundings, he begins to communicate with the other teachers as well as with the children. He is even heard to say "Sa!" once (for "sand"), much to Maria's amazement, when he wants her to play with him!

There's so much a child can learn about communication from a caring teacher!

Does Maria realize how much André has gained from his interaction with her? Maybe she doesn't give it much thought, once she sees how much happier he is. But if we take a closer look at how much André has gained, we can begin to appreciate just how important these day-to-day interactions are, not only to children's language learning, but to their feelings about themselves and about being in a child care environment.

When André was playing with Maria, he said the word "Sand" for the first time. He learned the word because Maria's comments and labels were expressed simply and clearly, which helped him figure out the meaning of the word. However, knowing a word isn't enough motivation for a child to use it. He has to have a reason or a purpose for using it and, in this case, André said, "Sand" because he really wanted Maria to play with him. It is the desire to interact with others which is the most powerful motivation for communicating.

Within his relationship with Maria, André felt safe. Her responsiveness gave him the motivation and the confidence to communicate both with her and with others in his strange, new environment.

This is the kind of environment all children in child care need, an environment where they are nurtured and provided with opportunities for positive, enjoyable interactions on and off throughout the day. This is the challenge facing you as an Early Childhood Educator.

B. Take a Closer Look at Children's Conversational Styles

Because communication skills are so closely linked to social skills, the best way to learn about how children communicate is to watch them interacting with others.

You are on the late shift, and you come into your preschool classroom at 10 a.m. during free play.

As you come in, Patrice runs up to you and shows you her new shoes. She says they are special because they glow in the dark. Then she calls to her friend and runs off.

Carlos, who is busy in the block centre, looks up briefly when you come in and then goes on playing alongside three other children. They are all very engrossed in their constructions.

Playing "Doctor" in the dramatic play centre, is a group of four children, who are having a heated discussion about what kind of treatment the "patient" needs.

Erin, who is playing alone as usual, pretends to feed her dolls and put them to bed. When you say hello to her and ask if her baby is tired, she says, "Yes. She gotta go to bed early." When you move on, you notice that her eyes follow you, and it seems that she really wanted you to stay and play.

Michael, who is developmentally delayed, stares into space, taking no notice of the other children. He doesn't respond when you say hello to him, but then he seldom responds when anyone talks to him.

All of these children react differently to you, and you probably react in different ways to each of them because of their different **conversational styles**.

Conversational styles evolve from the time a child is born. Each child is born with his or her own personality, and each caregiver has his or her own way of relating to a child, a way which is affected by what kind of personality the child has. In time, the child and caregiver develop a way of interacting with each other, like two dance partners coordinating their moves. Within these interactions, caregivers become the child's mirror, reflecting back their impressions of his ability to communicate. They give feedback on how well the child sent a message ("Oh, you want your bottle!" — the baby knows that this message was picked up loud and clear) and on whether the message was well-received ("What a big smile! You're such a happy little guy!" — this reaction tells him that smiles really get a positive reaction!).

Children's conversational styles evolve as they see themselves through other people's eyes and, in later childhood, as they compare themselves with others. From the thousands of interactions children have with their caregivers, siblings and peers, they gather internal "pictures" of themselves, which they paste in an imaginary photo album in their heads. From these pictures, they form their own views of themselves as communicators.

Patrice and the group playing "Doctor" look like confident communicators and seem to have positive internal pictures of themselves. And while Carlos isn't interactive when he's engrossed in his play, in general he seems to be a sociable, confident child.

However, Erin's style may be telling you that her internal picture is of someone who doesn't expect to get a positive response from others. And Michael's style seems to tell you that he hardly pictures himself as a communicator at all.

Taking a closer look at children's conversational styles gives us a better understanding of why some children communicate so naturally and why others find it so difficult.

The Four Conversational Styles

When looking at conversational styles, it is important to notice whether children spontaneously approach others and **initiate** interactions and how well they **respond** when others initiate interactions with them.

In general, you will notice that:

• Some children **initiate** interactions with ease — others don't.
• Some children **respond** readily during interactions — others don't.

By looking at how frequently children initiate and respond during interactions, we can identify four different **conversational styles** which describe the way a child interacts most of the time.

You can usually identify a child as having one of the following conversational styles (although often this will change from situation to situation):

1. The Sociable Child

2. The Reluctant Child

3. The Child with His Own Agenda

4. The Passive Child

Identifying the Four Conversational Styles

1. The Sociable Child

This child initiates interactions constantly and is very responsive to others' initiations. Even in infancy, sociable children initiate interactions to draw attention to themselves. Some sociable children interact freely in any situation, but others are more sociable with their peers than they are with their teachers or vice versa.

If language-delayed, the sociable child may be slow to talk or difficult to understand, but this doesn't deter him from interacting with others. However, he may be less socially mature than his peers.

2. The Reluctant Child

This child seldom initiates and is often on the outside of group activities and interactions. He may take a long time to "warm up" and respond to you when you approach him. However, given time and opportunities, he **will** interact with you. Peer interactions may be more difficult for him.

If language-delayed, this child's reluctance to initiate may be related to his language difficulty. He may be reluctant to interact with others because he can't make himself understood. Or, as a result of a language disorder, he may not yet have learned how to use his communication skills to interact appropriately in social situations. However, he usually responds when others make an effort to interact with him.

3. The Child with His Own Agenda

This child spends a lot of time playing alone, appearing to be uninterested in interaction. He may initiate when he needs something, but he frequently rejects your efforts to engage him. Normally-developing children may go through this independent phase when they want to "do their own thing." However, they still enjoy interacting with others in some social situations.

When a child has a significant delay in both social and communication development, this type of behaviour may not change much over time. His lack of social interaction may be due to the fact that he has not developed the necessary social skills for getting attention, for sharing information and for following another person's focus of interest. Interacting with this child may be extremely difficult.

4. The Passive Child

This child seldom responds or initiates, demonstrating little interest in the objects or people around him. It is hard to elicit a smile from him or to engage him in any sort of playful interaction. If this is the child's consistent style of interaction, it reflects a developmental delay.

Teachers Can't Help But Be Affected By Children's Conversational Styles

Think of the group of children you work with and ask yourself the following questions:

Which children do I enjoy interacting with the most?

What are their conversational styles?

Which children do I interact with the least?

What are their conversational styles?

You may or may not be surprised to discover that the children who get the most attention from you are the **sociable** children. But it's important to understand **why.**

They get attention from you because they **demand** it (in a very nice way, of course!). They initiate interactions with you all the time — and naturally you respond. They make you feel good because they are interesting and entertaining, and it's human nature to respond positively to people who make us feel good.

But what about the children who **don't** demand attention or who demand it in negative ways? Because these children are difficult to interact with, once again human nature comes into play — you have fewer interactions with them. They don't engage you, and you are less likely to engage them. And when you do interact with them, the interaction may be limited to talking about necessities. For example, you may talk to less interactive preschoolers at the lunch table only to ask whether they have finished eating or want more juice. By contrast, you and the sociable children talk non-stop about their families, their experiences, places they've visited etc. — a completely different kind of conversation.

> *The consequences for children of not being involved in frequent social interactions are obvious: the children have fewer opportunities than their sociable peers to learn language.*

The consequences for children of not being involved in frequent social interactions are obvious: the children have fewer opportunities than their sociable peers to learn language. In addition, their negative perceptions of themselves as communicators are confirmed. "I'm no good at communicating. That's why I can't get them to pay attention to me," they might think. What devastating consequences this can have!

So, it follows that children who are reluctant, passive or who have their own agenda need to become more active conversation partners. That's not so easy. In many cases this involves helping them change their view of themselves as communicators. That's where the teacher's role comes in...

C. Teachers Play Many Roles During Interactions with Children

The way you interact with children often depends on the child and the situation. Take a moment to think about some of the roles you play when you interact with children, because your role can make or break an interaction.

The Director Role

In this role, the teacher maintains tight control over the children and their activities. She spends much of her time making suggestions, giving directions and asking questions. This can make it very difficult for children to initiate and play an active role in interactions.

The Entertainer Role

In this role, the teacher is playful and lots of fun, but she does most of the talking and playing, giving the children few opportunities to take an active part in the interaction.

The Timekeeper Role

In this role, the teacher rushes through activities and routines in order to stay on schedule. This results in very limited interactions.

The Too-quiet Teacher Role

In this role, the teacher sits with the children, but hardly interacts with them, even when they initiate.

The Rescuer Teacher Role

In this role, the teacher assumes that the child won't be able to express himself, and so she talks for him or offers help before he has shown any need for it.

The Responsive Teacher Role

In this role, the teacher is tuned in to the children's needs and interests. She responds to each child in ways that encourage him to take an active part in interactions, both with her and with peers.

At different times you will find yourself playing different roles depending, for example, on the type of child you're interacting with, how many children are with you, their general behaviour, the time you have available and the mood you're in!

Which role do you play <u>most</u> of the time?

Teachers' Roles and Children's Styles Don't Always Match

When the teacher's role and the child's conversational style don't match, the teacher and child never really connect. Not only do they both feel frustrated but the child's potential for language learning is not fulfilled.

However, it's important to realize that the roles teachers play are significantly affected by the child's conversational style. When children aren't responsive and when they don't communicate spontaneously, it's natural to direct, question, entertain and even rescue them in an effort to get an interaction going. But it doesn't work! In fact, it can have the opposite effect because, very often, the child communicates even less.

Let's look at the thought processes of teachers and "hard-to-reach" children as the teachers try to make contact with them:

The director teacher and the passive child

The rescuer teacher and the reluctant child

The entertainer teacher and the child with his own agenda

The only role that consistently provides children with the encouragement and support they need in learning to communicate is the RESPONSIVE role.

In later chapters we'll discuss how to adopt this role with **all** children, regardless of their conversational styles.

D. Interactions with Peers: A Vital Part of Learning to Communicate

Playing with a mate helps children learn to communicate.

Let's take a look at André during outdoor play a few weeks after his arrival at Happy Days Child Care Centre. We find him and another little boy squealing with delight as they take turns climbing on to a step and making a big show of jumping down on to the ground.

We can see that the two boys are definitely interacting — they take turns jumping off the step, they look at one another as they jump, and then they laugh gleefully. They are obviously experiencing the special pleasure that comes from sharing an experience with a playmate.

Playing with peers is a wonderful, magical part of childhood. It's also a very important part of language learning, because what children learn from interacting with peers has an enormous impact on both their social and language development.

Peer interactions are different from adult-child interactions in a number of ways. One important difference relates to how the two conversation partners keep the interaction going. In adult-child interactions, the adult uses various strategies to help the child stay in the conversation. Because peers can't support a child's continued participation in an interaction the way an adult can, children have to learn to "hold their own" during interactions. When an interaction with peers goes wrong due to a conflict, a lack of interest or a misunderstanding, children have to know how to get things back on track. This is called "repairing" a breakdown in communication — and interactions with peers provide many opportunities for learning to do this.

Through peer interaction, children also develop the ability to see things from another person's point of view. They learn to make compromises, to resolve conflicts and to share, collaborate and cooperate with others. They also learn how to negotiate and assert themselves, which is an important skill. And all this is accomplished through the use of language.

Peer interaction becomes more and more dependent upon language as children's play skills develop. Some types of play can't succeed unless children have adequate language skills. In sociodramatic play, for example, children must be able to use language to plan, explain and negotiate as well as to create imaginary situations. These skills, which involve using certain kinds of vocabulary, grammatical forms and ways of expressing oneself, are learned during play with other children. Between 3 and 5 years, it becomes obvious that the children who interact most often with their peers are the ones who have excellent language skills.

> *Through peer interaction, children develop the ability to see things from another person's point of view. They learn to make compromises, to resolve conflicts and to share, collaborate and cooperate with others. They also learn how to negotiate and assert themselves, which is an important skill. And all this is accomplished through the use of language.*

Children who are developmentally delayed or language-delayed, children who are learning English as a second language or children who lack age-appropriate social skills will be at a serious disadvantage when it comes to peer interactions. If they don't have the language or the social skills to interact with their peers, they will find themselves left out. And when they are left out, they can't learn the social and language skills that are normally gained through peer interactions. In Chapter 6 we'll take a look at what you can do to support and encourage children's interactions with their peers.

E. Observing Peers at Play

Peer interaction usually takes place within play situations. Therefore, it is helpful to look at:

1. What types of play children engage in

2. How much social interaction takes place during the play

1. Types of Play Children Engage In

A. Functional Play

This type of play begins in the first year of life and peaks between 2 and 3 years of age.

Functional play reflects Piaget's category of sensorimotor play, during which the child performs repetitive motor movements, which include manipulating and exploring toys and objects in the environment.

Examples of functional play are:

• **performing various actions on a toy:** for example, banging or shaking blocks, or putting objects into a container and then taking them out.

• **cause-effect actions:** for example, switching lights or music boxes on and off, acting on busy boxes, seeing the effects of one's actions on sand, water, playdough etc.

• **using objects according to their real functions:** for example, pushing a car back and forth.

• **motor activities:** for example, running and jumping.

B. Constructive Play

This type of play begins in the second year of life and peaks between 3 and 4 years of age. It is still seen at 5 or 6 years of age.

During constructive play, the child uses materials to create or construct something from a plan he has in mind. The materials may be the same as those used for functional play, but he uses them to build something. For example, blocks are used to make a building or a tower. During constructive play, a child may spend a great deal of time on one activity, concentrating on achieving his goal.

C. Dramatic Play

This type of play begins in the second year and peaks between 6 and 7 years of age.

The child pretends during dramatic play. At first this consists of acting out real-life situations alone, using realistic props. In time, the pretense progresses to cooperative make-believe play in groups, where language is used to create the play setting and story. There is less dependence on objects, and the objects used in the play may look nothing like those they are supposed to represent.

D. Games with Rules

This type of play begins at about 6 years of age and continues throughout adulthood.

Children play games according to a set of rules which are accepted by the players — e.g., checkers, tag and kickball.

2. How Much Social Interaction Takes Place During the Play?

As you observe a child at play, look at how involved he is with the other children or how aware he seems of their presence. It is important to bear in mind that, even at the kindergarten level, children still spend some time playing alone:

A. No Play or Social Interaction

During free play, if you look around the room, you may notice some children who aren't playing at all. A child may be:

- **unoccupied** — the child doesn't play, but may watch others briefly or glance around, not focusing on one activity for very long. In general, he shows very little interest in any one activity.

- **an onlooker** — the child observes groups of children, without attempting to join in, although he may speak to them. This differs from being unoccupied because the child is showing a definite interest in what the other children are doing and positions himself close to them.

B. Solitary Play

No Social Interaction
The child plays alone, using toys which are different from those being used by children nearby.

Solitary-Functional play

C. Parallel Play

Minimal Social Interaction

Children play independently, but alongside one another, using the same toys and materials. They may look at each other's materials, make eye contact or imitate another child's actions, showing a definite awareness of each other's presence. Parallel play is thought to provide children with the right conditions to move on to more interactive forms of play.

D. Group Play

A Lot of Social Interaction

This includes:

- **associative play** — the children play with each other, each child pursuing his own interests within the same activity. They talk about what they are doing, exchange materials and follow each other around. They are involved in a similar type of play activity because of a common interest in the activity, not because of a desire to play cooperatively.

- **cooperative play** — the children play together in a group that is organized to achieve some goal, as in sociodramatic play or when playing a formal game. There is a sense of group cohesiveness, with one or two leaders assigning roles and responsibilities. The children cooperate and collaborate to accomplish the goal. Older and more mature children will be seen to engage in more associative and cooperative play.

Parallel-constructive play

Cooperative group-dramatic play

In the next section, we will see how children's play, social and language skills become integrated and enable them to participate in cooperative group interactions at the preschool stage.

Peer Interactions Improve with Age

As children mature and develop a wider range of play and social skills, their play with peers becomes more and more interactive. Therefore, we need to know what kinds of play we can expect from children at different ages and stages.

Infants (up to 18 months)

We can expect:

- **some unoccupied behaviour**
- **some onlooker behaviour**
- **solitary-functional play**
- **some solitary-dramatic play (in the second year)**
- **some solitary-constructive play (in the second year)**
- **some group-functional play (in the second year)**

Infants haven't yet developed the skills to engage in extended give-and-take interactions with a peer. Therefore, we can expect mostly individual play from infants.

However, infants **do** interact with their peers in functional play activities. They just do it far less often than older children do and these interactions are usually brief.

Infant teachers have described how babies little older than a year enjoy "running" from one side of the room to the other in a small group or how they all bang on the table at lunch (teachers' favourite!). It's obvious that these activities are social because the children actually look at one another, smile and laugh together, and during the running activity, they wait for one another before changing direction.

Infants enjoy interacting with peers during
(noisy) functional play activities!

Toddlers (18-30 months)

> **We can expect:**
>
> - **some unoccupied behaviour**
> - **some onlooker behaviour**
> - **solitary-functional play**
> - **solitary-dramatic play to increase**
> - **solitary-constructive play to increase**
>
> **There is a definite increase in the following:**
>
> - **parallel-functional play**
> - **parallel-constructive play**
> - **parallel-dramatic play**
> - **group-functional play (in the third year)**

Toddlers still engage in solitary play, but they spend about half of their play time in parallel play activities. Group play consists primarily of group-functional play, but the toddler now has a larger repertoire of interactions that can be shared with peers. This includes imitating another's actions (for example, when one child was observed to imitate another who was throwing all the books off the bookshelf; the game was cut short, needless to say!), playing turn-taking games such as run-and-chase, ball games, rough-and-tumble games and performing actions on the same toy.

Of course, in addition to these positive interactions, there are countless struggles to get the same toy or to become involved in the same activity, which can involve a fair amount of hitting, pushing, scratching and even the odd bite! Toddlers still have a lot to learn about life from the other guy's point of view.

Parallel-dramatic play is a common sight in the toddler room.

Preschoolers and Kindergartners (3-5 years)

We can expect:

- unoccupied behaviour to decrease
- solitary-functional play to decrease
- solitary-dramatic play to decrease
- parallel-functional play to decrease
- parallel-dramatic play to decrease

There is a definite increase in the following:

- mature solitary- or parallel-constructive play
- cooperative group play (sociodramatic play)

Solitary and parallel play decrease from 3-5 years of age, but they don't disappear. While solitary-functional and solitary-dramatic play should decrease, we still expect to see preschoolers and kindergartners engaged in solitary- or parallel-constructive play such as building, constructing or drawing. Even at 4½ years children spend about a third of their time in parallel play, which offers them the opportunity to be near their peers without having to be actively involved with them.

A qualitative difference can be seen in the parallel play of children who are approaching school age: it becomes more complex and involves more constructive play. It is quite common to see 4- and 5-year-olds sitting side by side doing puzzles, constructing with Lego, drawing or making something at the sand table. Children with the ability to concentrate on a construction or creation for a long time are thought to show independence, creativity and perseverance.

Solitary-constructive play is a common sight in the preschool room.

Group play often grows out of parallel-functional play as children start off by examining and manipulating sensory materials like sand and playdough and then proceed to play with the materials associatively or cooperatively. Parallel-functional play gives less sociable children the opportunity to work their way into a group by first playing alongside peers and then trying to gain entry into the group's play.

Group play, particularly cooperative group play, increases between 3 and 5 years of age. 3-3½-year-olds spend approximately one quarter of their time in group play and interact with their peers more frequently than with their teachers. Cooperative dramatic play becomes one of their preferred activities. By 5 years of age, children create pretend play scenarios and can interact with their peers for long periods of time.

F. When Is a Lack of Peer Interactions Cause for Concern?

By the time children reach the preschool stage, any difficulty with peer interactions becomes more and more obvious. While you can expect preschoolers to engage in solitary- and parallel-constructive play, there should still be an increase in cooperative group play and in verbal conversations with peers after 3 years of age. Not every child is outgoing and sociable, but most children do develop relationships with their peers after the age of 3 and are able to maintain social interactions for at least a short time.

From 3 years onwards, children should demonstrate most of the following behaviours with peers:

- getting a peer's attention
- being the leader in an activity
- imitating a peer
- expressing affection toward a peer
- expressing hostility toward a peer
- following or refusing to follow a peer's request
- negotiating an acceptable solution
- playing in a group for a relatively long time

As you can see, children need to be able to cooperate, as well as to assert themselves during peer interactions.

Preschoolers or kindergartners, like Erin on page 9, who engage only in solitary play need your help to move on to more interactive types of play. In other words, they need help getting in on the act.

If toddlers and, in particular, preschoolers spend large amounts of time unoccupied (like Michael on page 10), engaged in onlooker behaviour or in functional play activities, this may be cause for concern. In addition to following the suggestions outlined in Part 2 and Chapter 6 in particular, you are likely to need some outside help.

It's not easy for some children to get in on the act.

Summary

In child care, teachers are responsible for creating environments that build strong relationships and promote language learning. However, the interactions in child care are varied and complex. They depend on the child's conversational style, on the role the teacher plays and on the child's ability to play with peers. By being aware of how each partner in the interaction affects the other and of how peer interactions develop over time, teachers can observe the interactions in their classrooms to see whether or not each child's need for frequent, enjoyable interactions is being met. The knowledge gained from these observations helps teachers ensure that every child becomes a fully participating member of the group.

G. Introduction to Observation Guides

There are two Observation Guides in this book: one at the end of this chapter (Chapter 1) and one at the end of Chapter 2. Each Observation Guide is designed to help you use the information contained in the chapter so that you can observe individual children and become aware of their abilities and needs.

The Observation Guide in Chapter 1 (**"The Child's Interactions with Teachers and Peers"**) helps you identify the child's conversational style, the situations in which s/he is most and least interactive and her/his ability to engage in peer interactions.

The Observation Guide in Chapter 2 (**"The Child's Stage of Language Development"**) helps you identify the child's stage of language development and her/his ability to engage in social interactions. In addition, if the child is verbal, the guide will direct your observations of her/his expressive and receptive language skills.

If you are concerned about a child's ability to communicate, you are strongly recommended to complete these Observation Guides. In the chapters that follow, much of the information has been divided into sections which address the needs of children according to their stages of language development and to their conversational styles. Therefore, by completing these two Observation Guides, you will know which sections of the book are most relevant for individual children in your care.

Please note: All Observation Guide pages may be photocopied.

H. Observation Guide 1: The Child's Interactions with Teachers and Peers

Let's say that there is a child in your room whose language and social skills seem immature for his age. You might have noticed that he's very quiet and doesn't interact much with you or with peers. But perhaps if you observe him closely, you'll discover that there are situations in which he **does** interact. And while you know his weaknesses in his interactions with others, can you identify some of his strengths?

This guide is designed to help you take a closer look at a child's interactions in the child care setting. However, before you begin your observations, remember to:

1. Observe the child in many situations over an extended period.

A child's communication and interaction vary from day to day, from activity to activity and from conversation partner to conversation partner. Other factors can also have an impact on how much or how little s/he interacts: illness, lack of sleep and problems at home will all affect the child's desire and ability to communicate.

It is wise, therefore, to observe the child in many different situations, both indoors and outdoors, and to spread your observations over a number of days.

2. Consider the need for new or different kinds of materials and activities.

Consider whether the materials available in your room are appropriate to the child's age and interests and whether some new activities and materials might encourage more interaction and communication. A change of theme in the dramatic play area, for example, or a new sensory activity may arouse the child's interest and motivate her/him to share this interest with others.

Interaction Observation Guide 1: The Child's Interactions with Teachers and Peers

---

> Child's name:
>
> Age at time of this observation:
>
> Child's first language:
>
> Child's ability to speak English (if child is verbal) :
>
> Date:

1. Observe the child's conversational style

I think (child's name)_____'s conversational style is:

- ☐ **social** because s/he initiates and responds frequently to others' initiations

- ☐ **reluctant** because s/he seldom initiates, but does respond to others' initiations

- ☐ **own agenda** because s/he may initiate, but rarely responds to others' initiations and seems to prefer being alone

- ☐ **passive** because s/he hardly initiates or responds to others' initiations

  (you may want to check off more than one)

If the child's conversational style is reluctant, passive or own agenda, does s/he interact better with:

- ☐ Teachers
- ☐ Peers
- ☐ Neither

Observation Guide 1 (continued)

2. Observe the child's interactions with teachers

a) Names of teachers with whom s/he communicates with the most:

b) The situations in which s/he communicates and interacts willingly with a teacher:

c) The situations in which s/he communicates and interacts the LEAST with a teacher:

Observation Guide 1 (continued)

3. Observe the child's play interactions with peers

After referring to the examples on this page, use the sheet on the next page to write down a number of examples of the child's play interactions with peers.

Interactions with Peers During Play Activities				
	Functional	**Constructive**	**Dramatic**	**Games with Rules**
Solitary	Plays with music box near other children who are playing with puzzles	Building a tower. No children nearby	Plays alone, pretending to call someone on the phone	
Parallel	Driving cars on floor beside another child; not pretending or interacting	Building Lego construction on the floor along-side 3 children; not interacting	Pretending to cook for and feed a doll alongside another child; looking at each other, but not interacting	
Group	Chasing around the playground with 2 other children	Making a railway track with 3 other children	Playing "Doctor" cooperatively with 3 other children	Playing Snakes and Ladders with another child

	Unoccupied / Onlooking	**Activities**
Nonplay	Watching children in the house centre	Reading in the book centre next to another child

Adapted by Johnson, Christie and Yawkey (1987) from Sponseller and Lowry (1974)

Observation Guide 1 (continued)

Interactions with Peers During Play Activities			
	Functional	Constructive	Dramatic	Games with Rules
Solitary				
Parallel				
Group				

	Unoccupied / Onlooking	Activities
Nonplay		

Adapted by Johnson, Christie and Yawkey (1987) from Sponseller and Lowry (1974)

Observation Guide 1 (continued)

---

3. Observe the child's play interactions with peers (continued)

a) What types of play does the child engage in most of the time?

- ☐ Functional
- ☐ Constructive
- ☐ Dramatic
- ☐ Games with rules

b) How much social interaction takes place during the play?

☐ **No social interaction (Solitary Play)**

Most of the time, the child engages in the following kinds of solitary play:

- ☐ Solitary-functional
- ☐ Solitary-constructive
- ☐ Solitary-dramatic

☐ **Minimal social interaction (Parallel Play)**

The child plays alongside other children, using the same toys and materials as they do, showing an awareness of them, but not interacting with them. Most of the time, the child engages in the following kinds of parallel play:

- ☐ Parallel-functional
- ☐ Parallel-constructive
- ☐ Parallel-dramatic

☐ **A lot of social interaction (Group Play)**

The child interacts with other children, using the same materials as they do and engaging in conversation with them.

The group play is mainly:

- ☐ Associative (each child pursues his own interests)
- ☐ Cooperative (the group cooperates to achieve a goal)

Most of the time, the child engages in the following kinds of group play:

- ☐ Group-functional
- ☐ Group-constructive
- ☐ Group-dramatic

Observation Guide 1 (continued)

3. Observe the child's play interactions with peers (continued)

    c) With which children does the child interact most frequently?

    d) During which activities is the child MOST interactive with her/his peers?

    e) During which activities is the child LEAST interactive with her/his peers?

Observation Guide 1 (continued)

4. Summary of Observations

The following people, activities and situations seem to make communication and interaction more enjoyable or manageable for _____(child's name).

If you want to help a child become more interactive with both teachers and peers, read Part 2, Chapters 3,4,5 and 6.

References

Asher, S., Oden, S. & Gottman, J. (1977). Children's friendships in school settings. In L Katz (Ed.), *Current topics in early childhood education.* Norwood, NJ: Ablex.

Barnes, S., Gutfreund, M., Satterly, D. & Wells, G. (1983). Characteristics of adult speech which predict children's language development. *Journal of Child Language, 10,* 65-84.

Bell, R.Q. & Harper, L.V. (1977). *Child effects on adults.* Hillsdale, NJ: Erlbaum.

Briggs, D. C. (1975). *Your child's self-esteem.* New York: Doubleday.

Charlesworth, R. (1983). *Understanding child development.* Albany: Delmar.

Conti-Ramsden, G. (1985). Mothers in dialogue with language-impaired children. *Topics in Language Disorders, 5*(2), 58-68.

Ervin-Tripp, S. (1991). Play in language development. In B. Scales, M. Almy, A. Nicolopoulou & S. Ervin-Tripp (Eds.), *Play and the social context of development in early care and education* (pp. 84-97). New York: Teachers College Press.

Fey, M.E. (1986). *Language intervention with young children.* San Diego, CA: College Hill Press.

Ginsberg, H. & Opper, S. (1969). *Piaget's theory of intellectual development: An introduction.* Englewood Cliffs, NJ: Prentice Hall.

Guralnick, M. (1981). Peer influences on the development of communicative competence. In P. Strain (Ed.), *The utilization of classroom peers as behaviour change agents* (pp. 31-68). New York: Plenum.

Guralnick, M. (1990). Peer interactions and the development of handicapped children's social and communicative competence. In H. Foot, M.J. Morgan & R.H. Shute (Eds.) *Children helping children* (pp. 275-305). New York: John Wiley & Sons.

Halliday, M. (1975). *Learning how to mean.* London: Edward Arnold.

Johnson, J.E., Christie, J.F. & Yawkey, T.D. (1987). *Play and early childhood development.* Glenview, IL: Scott, Foresman.

La Greca, A.M. & Stark, P. (1986). Naturalistic Observations of children's social behaviour. In P.S. Strain, M. Guralnick & H.M. Walker (Eds.), *Children's social behaviour: Development, assessment and modification* (pp. 181-217). New York: Academic Press.

Lieven, E.M. (1978). Conversations between mothers and young children: Individual differences and their possible implication for the study of language learning. In N. Waterson & C. Snow (Eds.), *The development of communication* (pp. 173-187). Chichester: John Wiley & Sons.

McLean, J., & Snyder-McLean, L.A. (1978). *A transactional approach to early language training.* Columbus, Ohio: Charles E. Merrill.

Parten, M.B. (1932). Social participation among preschool children. *Journal of Abnormal and Social Psychology, 27,* 243-269.

Rubin, K.H. & Ross, H.S. (Eds.), (1982). *Peer relationships and social skills in childhood.* New York: Springer-Verlag.

Rubin, K. (1986). Play, peer interaction and social development. In Gottfried, A.W. and C. Caldwell Brown (Eds.), *Play interactions: The contribution of play materials and parental involvement to children's development.* Proceedings of the eleventh Johnson and Johnson Pediatric Round Table (pp.163-174). Lexington, Mass: Lexington Books.

Smilansky, S. & Shefatya, L. (1990). *Facilitating play: A medium for promoting cognitive, socio-emotional and academic development in young children.* Gaithersburg, MD: Psychosocial and Educational Publications.

Snow, C.E. (1984). Parent-child interaction and the development communicative ability. In R.L. Schiefelbusch & J. Pickar (Eds.), *The acquisition of communicative competence* (pp. 69-107). Baltimore: University Park Press.

Sponseller, D. & Lowry, M. (1974) Designing a play environment for toddlers. In D. Sponseller (Ed.), *Play as a learning medium* (pp. 81-109). Washington, DC: National Association for the Education of Young Children.

Tiegerman, E. & Siperstein, M. (1984). Individual patterns of interaction in the mother-child dyad: Implications for parent intervention. *Topics in Language Disorders, 4*(4), 50-61.

Tomlinson-Keasy, C. (1985). *Child development: Psychological, sociocultural and biological factors.* Homewood, IL: The Dorsey Press.

Wetherby, A. (1991). *Profiling communication and symbolic abilities: Assessment and intervention guidelines.* Presentation at Toronto Children's Centre, Toronto, Ontario.

C H A P T E R   2

The Stages of Language Development: Talking Takes Time

A. An Amazing Five-Year Journey: From "Waaaaa!" to "When I grow up, I wanna be a pilot."

In five short years, normally-developing children make incredible progress in their ability to use language. They progress from using **nonverbal communication** (sending messages through sounds, actions, eye gaze, facial expression and gestures) to using **verbal communication** or **spoken language,** which is the most complex skill human beings develop.

Although most babies say their first words at about 14 months, they start learning about communication right from birth. The foundations of both communication and turn-taking develop in that critical first year.

Once children begin to talk, they still have a lot to learn about language and how to use it. Comprehension, conversational skills, grammar, vocabulary and the ability to use language as a tool for thinking and learning take years to develop and refine.

In order to know what to expect from children at each stage and how to help them progress to the next stage, you will need to become familiar with all the stages of language learning.

But before you learn about the stages of language development, it's important to understand **why** people communicate.

B. Children, Like Adults, Communicate for Many Different Reasons

Children have to learn to use language in many different situations and for many different reasons. Therefore, we can't look at HOW children communicate without becoming aware of WHY they communicate.

While communication enables us to draw attention to our physical needs, the most important reason for communicating is to satisfy our social needs. Human beings have an overwhelming need to connect with others and to share feelings, ideas and experiences. Whether we are happy, sad, excited or frustrated, we have a need to talk to someone about it.

Language has another critical function. It is a tool for thinking and learning. With language, we can consider alternatives, reason, imagine, plan, predict and solve problems.

To become aware of **why** you communicate, think back to the telephone calls you made over the past few days. You probably had a number of reasons for making those calls. Think about why you made the calls, and then think about why infants and children communicate. You will find many similarities.

Why People Communicate

1. To make a request

2. To protest about something (complain, reject)

3. To greet or take leave of someone

4. To respond to another person's communication

5. To ask for information (question)

6. To think, plan and problem-solve

7. To share feelings, ideas and interests

An awareness of **why** children communicate and of the importance of social interaction helps you decide what kind of support each child needs from you.

For example, a 2½-year-old who communicates only when she needs help must become involved in playful, social interactions if she is to learn to use language as a social tool.

By contrast, a sociable 3-year-old who speaks in jumbled sentences and is difficult to understand will need a different kind of support. Since this child readily engages you in social interactions, your focus during these interactions will be on providing her with language models that help her learn more mature ways of expressing herself.

C. The Seven Stages of Communication and Language Development

The following pages describe seven stages that normally-developing children go through as they develop language:

Stage 1

Birth to 3 months
The infant communicates reflexively

Stage 2

3 to 8 months
The infant is interested in others, but doesn't communicate intentionally

Stage 3

8 to 13 months
The infant communicates intentionally and becomes very sociable

Stage 4

12 to 18 months
The infant cracks the language code and uses her first words

Stage 5

18 to 24 months
The child uses two-word sentences and language development takes off!

Stage 6

24 to 36 months
The child uses three-word sentences, four-word sentences, five-word sentences...

Stage 7

3 to 5 years
The child uses long, complex sentences and can hold conversations

Children who are language-delayed take longer to achieve these stages of language development.

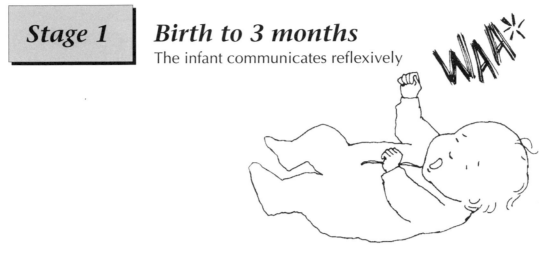

Stage 1	*Birth to 3 months*

The infant communicates reflexively

Why the child communicates

- **Communication is not intentional, but caregivers respond as if it were**
The infant does not perform actions with a goal in mind. He has no idea that his behaviour can affect others and cause them to behave in certain ways.

   You (the caregiver) respond to the infant's actions, sounds, eye gaze and even to burps, sneezes and coughs as if he **had** communicated with you for a reason.

   For example, if the infant happens to look toward a mobile, you might say "Oh, you want to see that mobile move," and you wind it up. Your responsiveness is what will eventually (at around 8 months) lead him to conclude "Hey! When I behave in certain ways, it makes people do things!"

How the child communicates

- **The infant responds reflexively**
The infant's behaviour consists of reflexive responses to his bodily needs and to things in the environment — e.g., he cries in response to hunger, startles in response to noise.

   By 2-3 months, you can see changes in his reflexive behaviour. For example, the sucking reflex now occurs when he sees the nipple and anticipates being fed — and not only when the nipple is put in his mouth.

Social interaction

- **Turn-taking games start early**
By 6 weeks, the baby is making cooing noises when he is in a settled state. By two months, the cooing increases and you can get him to coo just by talking animatedly to him (especially in a high-pitched voice) or by making sounds with a squeeze toy.

   When you and the infant are face-to-face, you smile at one another and make cooing sounds back and forth. And a lifetime of turn-taking begins.

Stage 1	HOW the infant behaves	Caregiver's interpretation of WHY the infant is communicating
	Cries, fusses, looks or moves away	To protest, reject, show distress/displeasure
	Looks, smiles, makes vowel-like sounds	To request action/object
	Looks, makes sounds, smiles, body movements, voice changes (loudness and pitch)	To respond to/show awareness of and interest in others

Stage 2 | *3 to 8 months*

The infant is interested in others, but doesn't communicate intentionally

Why the child communicates

- **Communication is still not intentional**
  The infant still does not realize that she can send a message directly to you in order to make something happen. You are still interpreting her behaviour as if she has a reason for behaving in a particular way.

How the child communicates

- **Actions, sounds and facial expressions make the child's behaviour easier to interpret**
  The infant's ability to move toward and to reach for objects makes it much easier for you to figure out what she wants. If she reaches for a closed container, bangs it, makes sounds at it and keeps turning it over, you know she wants to open it, even though she doesn't look at you and make sounds in your direction.

Stage 2

She also lets you know how she feels about what's going on. She makes sounds which communicate pleasure, displeasure, anger, contentment or eagerness to get something (such as "Uh! Uh!" when food appears). These sounds are usually easy to interpret, especially since they are accompanied by facial expressions and body movements.

- **Babbling begins**
  By six or seven months, she is babbling, and you hear long strings of consonants and vowels repeated endlessly — e.g., "dadadadadadada." This is the stage when babies make sounds to themselves in the mirror.

Social interaction

- **The child obviously wants your attention**
  In many situations, you can see that the child has a definite interest in getting or maintaining your attention. By 4 months, she does this by looking at you, smiling and making sounds in your direction. You respond to her as if she had actually called you, and you might say "So you want to talk to me, do you?" You have long "conversations" with her as you make sounds back and forth to each other.

- **Games like "Peek-a-boo" are a hit**
  The infant is easily engaged in social routines like "Peek-a-boo" and "Row, Row, Row Your Boat" and smiles and laughs happily as you play them with her. She takes her turn by making sounds or by moving her body to let you know that she wants the game to continue.

- **The child becomes interested in toys you show her**
  The infant can now focus on an object you show her. At about 6 months, as her interest in toys increases, her eye contact with you may actually **decrease** until she learns how to coordinate looking both at you **and** at the object she is playing with.

Language Development
Receptive Language

- **Understanding of words occurs only in context**
  At this stage, children can't understand words, but they can understand gestures, intonation and the general situation. For example, you say "Do you want to go for a walk?" as you pick her up and point towards the stroller. She gets very excited because she knows she's going for a walk. But she's understanding only the **nonverbal** cues; the words themselves have no meaning yet.

Stage 2	*HOW the infant sends messages*	*Caregiver's interpretation of WHY the infant is communicating*
	Cries, fusses, looks or moves away	To protest, reject, show distress/ displeasure
	Looks at what/whom she wants, reaches, moves towards, makes a variety of consonant and vowel sounds	To request action/object
	Looks at person, makes sounds, smiles, body movements, changes loudness and pitch of voice	To respond to/show awareness of and interest in others
	Makes sounds or performs action related to routine — e.g., rocks back and forth to request "Row, Row Your Boat."	To request social play routine **(new development)**
	Looks, makes sounds, babbles — e.g., "gagaga", changes loudness and pitch of voice, smiles, body move- ments	To call for attention **(new development)**

Stage 3	*8 to 13 months*

The infant communicates intentionally and becomes very sociable

Why the child communicates

- **Communication is clearly intentional — the child communicates with a goal in mind**

  The child understands the connection between his behaviour and your responses. He now realizes that if he wants or needs to accomplish something, the best thing to do is to communicate directly to you. He has many reasons for communicating: to make requests, to get your attention, to show you things and to greet you — to name a few.

How the child communicates

- **The child communicates using conventional gestures and is easier to understand**

  The child now uses conventional, recognizable gestures such as pointing, shaking his head and waving. By 9 months, he is able to combine gestures with sounds and eye gaze, which makes it easier for you to understand what he is trying to communicate.

  At 11-12 months, if he wants something, he may:

  — point and look at the object he wants; and

  — make a sound; and

  — look at you; and

  — look back at the object; and

  — look back at you; and finally,

  — repeat the sound

  That's pretty clear, isn't it? And just in case for some reason you don't respond, he won't give up!

Stage 3

At 11-12 months, if you are not responding when he communicates, he may:

> — add to his message by making a different sound
>
> — change the message by repeating it loudly
>
> — throw a tantrum (which usually gets a response!)

- **The child uses certain sounds as if they were words**
  At this stage, the child has very few single words, but may consistently use sounds that have a specific meaning in his mind — e.g. "Guh!" may mean "Look at that!"

  He may also show the beginnings of **question-asking,** which he does by pointing to something and making a sound with a questioning intonation. This could mean "What's that?" or "Who's there?", as an example.

- **Jargon appears: "It sounds like he's saying something, but I can't understand a word of it!"**
  The child produces long strings of sounds which have adult-like intonation patterns and, therefore, sound like questions, statements or commands. But these strings of sounds aren't real words, even though at times it sounds as if they are.

- **The child imitates an adult's sounds**
  If you make a babbling sound or even a noisy sound like "Vroom-vroom" to the child, he will imitate you, and the two of you will take turns back and forth for a very long time. You'll probably quit first — it takes a long time for a baby to get tired of this game!

Social interaction

- **Communication is used primarily for social reasons**
  The child spontaneously communicates with you to draw attention to himself and to draw attention to things of interest around him. Much of the time he communicates because he wants the pleasure of your company.

- **The child is now able to share his caregiver's focus and to get her to follow his focus**
  When the child is approximately 9 months, you can point to something and he will follow your point. In addition, if you are close to him he will notice when you turn to look at something and he will follow your line of vision.

  He has also learned to get you to focus on what he is focused by pointing, making sounds and looking at you. This enables him to establish **joint attention**, which is critical for language development because language is learned in the context of sharing information.

  By establishing joint attention, the child creates the ideal conditions for language learning because chances are that every time he points something out to you, you respond and provide him with a label.

Stage 3

- **The child takes turns in play situations**
When you're interacting with him, he'll use eye contact, actions, sounds and gestures to take his turn. Particularly during social routines like "Row, Row, Row Your Boat" or during play with toys, the child will enjoy taking turns with you. Making sounds and handing objects back and forth are very popular games at this stage.

Language development
Receptive Language

- **True comprehension of words has not yet developed**
The child *seems* to understand much of what is said to him and even seems to follow some directions, but by 13 months his comprehension of words is probably limited to a few labels of people or objects. He continues to make use of very clear clues both from your actions, intonation and from the situation itself.

For example, when he has had enough of fingerpainting and shows you that his hands are full of paint, you say to him "Clean your hands in the water" (you have a pail next to the table), and you gesture toward the pail. He goes over to the pail and washes his hands in the water.

His ability to follow your directions is a result of the context (he's used to washing his hands in the pail), your intonation and your gesture toward the pail.

WHY the child communicates (communication is now intentional)	HOW the child communicates
To direct or control another's behaviour Protests Requests action/object	Cries, moans Points, gestures
To interact for social purposes Requests social routine Calls for attention Requests comfort Shows off Greets	Pantomimes Sounds that have special meaning Makes eye contact
To establish joint attention (new to Stage 3) Draws attention to objects/events/people in environment Labels Requests information	Combination of pointing, looking and making sounds Single words

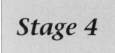

Stage 4 | *12 to 18 months*

The infant cracks the language code and uses her first words

Language development

Expressive Language

- **The child uses a small number of single words (about 10-20)**
  The child's first words refer to people, objects or events in the here-and-now that are of great interest to her. This includes words that capture change or movement (e.g., "Up" and "Gone"), as well as objects on which the child performs actions (e.g., "Book").

  Sometimes sounds that have been used consistently in certain situations evolve into first words (e.g., "Nananana", which was used to protest or reject something, may turn into the word "No"; and "Mmmmmm", which was used while reaching for more food, may turn into "More").

  Some words are simplified versions of the adult word (e.g.,"Baba" may mean "Bottle").

  Vocabulary increases slowly at first (she's working really hard on learning to walk at this time!).

- **One word may have different meanings in different contexts**
  The child will use the same word for different reasons.

    For example, "Mama" could mean:

      "Is that Mama's purse?" (question); or

      "There you are, Mama." (comment); or

      "Pick me up, Mama." (request)

  The context, gestures and body language the child uses provide the clues.

Stage 4

- **The child's use of a word is often too broad or too narrow**
  The child may use a word in one situation only (e.g.,"Baba" may refer only to her own bottle; not to another child's bottle or to a different shaped bottle). This is known as **underextension.**

  The child's use of the word may also go way beyond the conventional use (e.g.,"dog" may be used to describe all animals with four legs). This is known as **overextension**, which reflects children's association of objects, animals or people with similar visual characteristics.

  These extensions are adjusted as the child comes to realize that her word-use is inaccurate. When she learns the word "cow," for example, she realizes that "dog" doesn't apply to all four-legged animals. So she revises her use of the word "dog".

Receptive Language

- **The child begins to develop a receptive vocabulary**
  The child understands words that label familiar people and objects even when no cues are given. This signals that she has begun to comprehend spoken language

Social interaction

- **The child communicates for the same reasons as she did at Stage 3 — i.e., primarily for *social* reasons**
  Single words don't appear out of nowhere. Words provide the child with a more sophisticated way of sending messages that, till now, have been sent by means of nonverbal communication. For example, instead of pointing, looking at you and making sounds to draw your attention to a baby, the child now points and says "Baba."

- **The child perseveres if not responded to**
  If the child communicates and isn't responded to, she repeats herself, alters the message or finds another way to get her message across. This strategy of **"repair"** of a breakdown in communication is a very important one, since it plays a critical role in helping her find better ways of expressing herself.

Stage 5 | *18 to 24 months*

The child uses two-word sentences and language development takes off

Language development
Expressive Language

- **Two-word sentences begin**
  When the child has about 50 words, he may begin to combine single words into two-word sentences. In part, this is a result of his increased memory and ability to process information. However, he will still use single words much of the time.

  Two-word sentences may be used by children as young as 16 months, but many children don't begin to use them until after their second birthday.

- **One sentence can have different meanings in different situations**
  A two-word sentence, such as "Mommy car" may mean:

  "That's Mommy's car"; or "Mommy, I want to go in your car"; or "I went home in Mommy's car."

  Initially, the child may reverse word order (e.g.,"Car mommy"), but soon he will use the conventional word order.

- **Vocabulary undergoes a growth spurt**
  The child's vocabulary increases to about 200 words. Teachers of toddlers find themselves saying "I can't believe how much he's talking now — and it's just happened within the last few weeks!"

- **Negatives are used**
  The child expresses negatives by using "no" or "not," usually at the beginning of the sentence.

  For example, "No juice" or "Not wet."

Stage 5

- **Questions, questions and more questions are asked**
  Children at this stage can't ask grammatically correct questions, but by using a questioning intonation, they ask many questions that require a "Yes" or "No" answer. For example, "Dat my car?" would clearly be understood as a question just from the way the child's voice rises at the end of the sentence.

  He also uses question words like "Where?" and "What dat?"

  Questions are an important tool for language learning. If the adult's response to the question is appropriate to the child's language level, the child stands to learn a great deal from it.

- **Language is used to talk about more than the here-and-now**
  At first, spoken language is used to talk about the here-and-now. As the child's language improves, he will talk about past events and even about things that he knows will happen in the future.

Receptive Language

- **Comprehension improves**
  The child can now understand many words out of context. If you say "Let's go and wash your hands" when you are neither standing near a sink nor pointing to his hands, he will still understand what you mean (and that makes your job a lot easier).

  He understands a number of simple directions (e.g., "Kiss the baby") and can respond appropriately when asked to point to pictures in a book (e.g., "Show me the lion"). He also understands simple questions (e.g., "Where's your blanket?").

Social interaction

- **You can have brief conversations together**
  The child is beginning to take part in real (but brief) conversations. He will provide new information about a topic you have introduced or will ask a question about what you have said.

  Teacher: *That's a nice sweater, Gregory!*

  Gregory: *Bike. (Points at picture of a bike on his sweater)*
  — **new information**

  Teacher: *You've got a bike on your sweater! Wow!*

  Much of the time, however, the child neither answers your questions nor responds to your comments. It may sometimes feel as if you are talking to the wall, but that's because he is still learning how to become a conversationalist!

Stage 6 | *24 to 36 months*

The child uses three-word sentences, four-word sentences, five-word sentences. . . .

Baby dink milk.

Language development
Expressive Language

- **Three-word sentences develop, and sentence length continues to increase**

  When approximately half of the child's sentences contain two words, she begins to use three-word sentences.

  There are two types of three-word sentences:

  a) Combinations of two two-word sentences

  > For example, "Mommy drive" and "Drive car" become "Mommy drive car."

  b) Expansions of or additions to existing sentences

  > For example, "Eat cookie," becomes "Eat <u>big</u> cookie."

  > "A doggie" becomes "<u>That</u> a doggie."

- **Sentences become more grammatically correct**
  — PREPOSITIONS such as "in" and "on" are used.

  — VERBS become more complex:

  - verbs have -ing added to them

    > For example, "Mommy go" becomes "Mommy go<u>ing</u>."

  - verbs such as "gonna," "gotta," and "wanna" are used as if they were one word, because the child doesn't realise that they are a combination of two words. For example, "I <u>wanna</u> play."

  - "helping" or auxilliary verbs such as "can" and "will" and various forms of the verb "to be" such as "am," "are," and "is" are used after 2½ years.

Stage 6

For example, "He play too" becomes "He <u>can</u> play too."

"You going home" becomes "You <u>is</u> going home."

(These verbs can be very confusing to children and, at first, are often used incorrectly.)

— PLURALS are expressed by adding "s" to words. Until this stage, the child either didn't indicate plurals at all or used the word "more" to indicate that she was referring to more than one thing.

For example, "Look at my car" (holding two cars) becomes "Look at my car<u>s</u>."

— ARTICLES "the" and "a" appear, but take time to be used correctly.

For example, "That kitty" becomes "That <u>a</u> kitty" and later "Kitty go meow" becomes "<u>The</u> kitty go meow."

— PRONOUNS are now used when the child talks about herself, even though her use may be ungrammatical.

For example, "Dana want cookie" becomes "<u>Me</u> want cookie."

Pronouns such as "he," "she," "they," and "we" take a while to master.

When you speak to the children, you don't need to refer to yourself by name any more. You can say "<u>I'll</u> fix it for you," and they will know to whom "I" refers.

— NEGATIVES include "can't" and "don't, in addition to "no" and "not" and are now used in the <u>middle</u> of the sentence.

For example, "No want spoon!" becomes "I <u>don't</u> want spoon!"

— CONJUNCTION "and" is used to list two things together

For example, "I got candy <u>and</u> cake."

• **Children begin to ask "Why?"**
Those wonderful "Why?" questions are heard a lot although the child doesn't fully understand what "Why?" means. When you ask her a "Why?" question, she probably won't be able to answer it (especially if you ask something like "Why did you do that?" when she's just hit her best friend). She will learn what "Why?" means from your answers to her "Why?" questions.

• **The child becomes a storyteller**
She begins to tell little stories and uses language imaginatively and to express feelings. Her stories may be disjointed and hard to follow.

| Stage 6 | **Receptive Language** |

- **Comprehension grows and expands**

  By 3 years, the child understands many different concepts — e.g., "in-out," "big-little," "go-stop," "animals," "toys," including prepositions such as "under," "over," "in front of," "behind," "top," "bottom," etc.

  She can follow two-part directions — e.g., "Take your cup and put it in the sink."

  She can also follow simple stories in books.

Social interaction

- **Conversations go on for longer**

  By 3 years, the child can take a number of turns in a conversation, but it's easier for her to discuss something **she** has initiated than something you initiate. She also knows that a pause in the conversation is a signal for her to take her turn.

| Stage 7 | **3 to 5 years** |

The child uses long, complex sentences and can hold conversations

I showed Cindy my picture and she put it on the wall!

Language development
Expressive Language

- **The child links two ideas together in a complex sentence**

  As soon as most of the child's sentences are more than four words long, he begins to use complex sentences which consist of two or more ideas linked together. As a result, sentences may be twice as long as they were before.

Stage 7

At first, "and" is used to link two sentences together.

> For example, "My mommy's gonna buy me a car <u>and</u> my grandma's gonna buy me Lego."

After "and", the child will use "and then," "because," "what," "when," "but," "that," "if" and "so" to link ideas. This provides the child with endless possibilities for expressing herself.

> For example, "I can't walk <u>because</u> I got a sore leg."

> For example, "My baby's gonna sleep <u>when</u> she's tired <u>and then</u> I'll put her to bed."

Sentences contain verbs such as "think," "wish," "wonder," "hope," "remember," "pretend."

> For example, "I <u>think</u> I have one" or "<u>Pretend</u> you're the doctor."

- **The child's grammar becomes more complex**
  - — PRONOUNS such as "I," "you," "he," "she," "we," and "they" are used correctly

  - — QUESTIONS sound more like adults' questions

    - By 3½ years, the child has learned to reverse the order of the verb and noun to ask questions

      > For example,"What you are doing?" becomes "What <u>are you</u> doing?"

    - "Helping" or auxiliary verbs such as "are," "is," "can, "do," and "will" are used in questions

      > For example, "You help me? becomes "<u>Will</u> you help me?"

      > "He sick?" becomes "<u>Is</u> he sick?"

  - — NEGATIVES

    - By 3½ years the child uses more advanced forms of negatives — e.g., "doesn't" and "isn't." After 4 years, "nobody," "no one," "none" and "nothing" become part of the child's vocabulary.

    - By 4 years, the child can use "don't," "can't," "isn't" in the past tense — e.g., "I <u>didn't</u> do it!", "It <u>wasn't</u> my fault!", "I <u>couldn't</u> find it!" — which really helps him make up excuses!

- **The child's speech still contains many normal developmental errors**
  It takes time for the child to correct his grammatical errors. These normal errors reflect the child's attempts to find a general rule which can be applied to all words in a certain grammatical context.

Stage 7

For example, in the past tense, if you say "I call<u>ed</u>," "I shout<u>ed</u>," "I wash<u>ed</u>," and "I climb<u>ed</u>," why not say "I runn<u>ed</u>"?

Or if you say "That's hi<u>s</u>," "That's her<u>s</u>," "That's our<u>s</u>," "That's their<u>s</u>," and "That's your<u>s</u>" to indicate ownership or possession, why not say "That's mine<u>s</u>"?

- **The child's vocabulary is approaching 5000 words**
  Wow!

- **Language has become a tool for thinking, learning and imagining**
  Language is used as a tool for learning, organizing, thinking, problem-solving and creating. The child uses language to direct his own and others' behaviour, to plan what he's going to do, to anticipate what will happen, to report on things he's experiencing or has experienced in the past and to create imaginary situations.

Receptive Language

- **Comprehension becomes quite advanced: he seems to understand everything!**
  By 5 years, the child can follow stories and understand complex questions such as "What would happen if there was no rain?" or "How many ways can you think of to sort these buttons?"

Social interaction

- **Conversations continue for longer and the child can hold his own**
  You can tell that the child now understands more about the "rules" of conversation. He takes turns for a longer time, even on topics that are initiated by you. He even says "Yeah" or nods to acknowledge what you are saying, and he is well aware of the importance of a pause as a signal for a change in speaker.

  However, he may not give you a turn, especially when he's telling you something of great interest to him. (You have to be a good listener!) Sometimes he doesn't respond to the topic you've introduced — he switches to a topic in which he's interested.

  He's learned that to get into a conversation he has to be persistent. He knows that he has to get the listener's attention before he starts talking, and he does this by calling (or yelling out) the name again and again. During the conversation, he stays close to the listener and maintains eye contact to keep her attention.

- **Stories (narratives) become a regular part of the child's conversation**
  Stories or narratives involve a description of one or more past events. This includes describing events from the child's own experience, as well as telling imaginary stories.

  At 3 years, children tell short stories (often just one or two sentences), generally about very recent events. 3-year-olds seldom provide enough

Stage 7

background information for the listener to understand the story. You will probably find yourself asking questions to find out exactly who or what the story is about.

At 4 years, the picture changes quite dramatically. Stories are longer (they could be as long as four or five complex sentences), and the narrative is likely to be about an event in the past.

When telling the story, the child usually:

— introduces the story *("You know what happened to my Mom?")*

— provides background information *("Well, she was driving to work...")*

— provides information about what happened *("...and she saw this building was on fire...")*

— provides information about how the story ended *("...and the fireman came and put the fire out.")*

At 5 years, the changes are less striking, with children providing the listener with more details about the setting of the story and consistently "ending" the story with a final outcome or some description or evaluation of the situation.

For example: *"Anthony knocked down Shane's tower, and Shane got mad. So he pushed Anthony, and he fell and hurt his leg, and now they're both crying"* (story ending).

Summary

Communication begins at birth and continues to develop throughout childhood and early adulthood. In infancy, children learn that their behaviour has an effect on others, and from that realization evolves intentional (but still nonverbal) communication, which forms the foundation for all future communication. Even in infancy, children discover the power and pleasure of **social** communication, and within their day-to-day exchanges with caregivers, they learn language. Spoken language develops and is refined between the ages of one and five, by which time children are able to have lengthy conversations and use language to gain information, to think and to imagine. Children who are language-delayed take longer to achieve the stages of language development and their speech is frequently less mature than that of normally-developing children.

D. Observation Guide 2: The Child's Stage of Language Development

This Observation Guide will help you identify:

- the child's stage of language development
- her/his ability to engage in social interactions

Child's name:
Age at time of this observation:
Child's first language:
Child's ability to speak English (if child is verbal) :
Date:

For Children at Stages 1,2 and 3 (before language develops)

a) How often and for what reasons the child communicates
Observe the child in many different situations over a period of days to see HOW OFTEN s/he communicates for the reasons listed below. This will give you an idea of how often s/he communicates for social and for non-social reasons.

WHY \ HOW OFTEN	Often	Sometimes	Rarely	Never
• To protest				
• To request object or action				
• To request social routine				
• To call for attention				
• To respond to you when you talk to her/him				
• To request comfort				
• To show off or draw attention to self				
• To draw attention to people, things, events				
• To label (says a word)				
• To request information (by using questioning intonation)				

Observation Guide 2 (continued)

b) The child's stage of language development

When the child communicates, note HOW s/he sends his/her message and WHY s/he is communicating — then check the column where the HOW and WHY intersect.

WHY / HOW	To protest	To request action/ object	To respond to others	To request social routines e.g., Peek-a-boo	To call for attention	To request comfort	To show off	To draw attention to objects, people	To label	To ask for information
STAGE 1										
Cries, fusses										
Looks										
Smiles										
Makes vowel-like sounds										
Changes pitch, loudness of voice										
Body movements										
STAGE 2										
Changes facial expressions										
Laughs										
Makes a variety of consonant and vowel sounds										
Reaches/moves towards										
STAGE 3										
Looks at person to make eye contact										
Points										
Gestures e.g., waves, shakes head										
Pantomimes (acts out what s/he wants to say)										
Combines pointing, eye contact and making sounds										
Makes sounds that have special meaning										
Single words										

Observation Guide 2 (continued)

■

c) Social interaction

- ☐ takes turns making sounds back and forth
- ☐ has a definite interest in getting your attention
- ☐ is easily engaged when you play games like "Peek-a-boo"
- ☐ initiates games like "Peek-a-boo" and "Pat-a-Cake"
- ☐ draws attention to her/himself and to things in the environment
- ☐ can share your focus and get you to attend to what s/he's interested in by using eye contact, sounds, gestures, actions and by pointing
- ☐ interacts with you during play with toys

Summary of Observations for Children at Stages 1, 2 and 3

a) Child's stage of language development_____

b) Her/his ability to communicate and take turns seems to be:

- ☐ above age level
- ☐ at age level
- ☐ slightly below age level
- ☐ well below age level

Comments:

Observation Guide 2 (continued)

For Children at Stages 4, 5, 6 and 7 (after language develops)

a) Expressive Language

The child speaks using:

- [ ] single words
- [ ] two-word sentences
- [ ] three-word sentences plus
- [ ] long, complex sentences

The child's grammar seems to be:

- [ ] at age level
- [ ] a little below her/his age level
- [ ] quite delayed

The child uses the following kinds of questions:

- [ ] statements with a rising intonation e.g., "I have some?"
- [ ] Where, What, Who questions
- [ ] Why questions
- [ ] When, How questions
- [ ] no questions heard

The child uses language to:

- [ ] make requests
- [ ] talk about the here-and-now
- [ ] talk about the here-and-now, as well as past and future events
- [ ] think, plan, negotiate and imagine
- [ ] tell stories

b) Receptive Language

The child can understand:

- [ ] a few words that label familiar people and objects
- [ ] a fairly large number of words and simple directions (without any gestures or clues)
- [ ] many different ideas and concepts, two-part directions and short stories
- [ ] abstract concepts, complex questions, stories with a plot

Observation Guide 2 (continued)

c) Social Interaction

Your conversations with the child:

- ☐ are difficult to keep going and rarely last for more than one or two turns
- ☐ last longer when the child initiates them
- ☐ are very short, but s/he will respond to your comments/questions
- ☐ last for about three or four turns each, and longer if s/he initiated the conversation
- ☐ can go on for quite a long time

Summary of Observations for Children at Stages 4, 5, 6 and 7

a) Child's stage of language development_____

b) Expressive Language seems to be:
- ☐ above age level
- ☐ at age level
- ☐ slightly below age level
- ☐ well below age level

c) Receptive Language seems to be:
- ☐ above age level
- ☐ at age level
- ☐ slightly below age level
- ☐ well below age level

d) Social interaction seems to be:
- ☐ above age level
- ☐ at age level
- ☐ slightly below age level
- ☐ well below age level

Comments:

References

Bloom, L. & Lahey, M. (1978). *Language development and language disorders.* John Wiley & Sons.

Bowerman, M. (1979) The acquisition of complex sentences. In P. Fletcher & M. Garman, (Eds.), *Language acquisition* (pp. 285-306). Cambridge: Cambridge University Press.

Brown, R. (1983). *A first language: The early stages.* Cambridge: Harvard University Press.

Bruner, J. (1974/1975). From communication to language — A psychological perspective. *Cognition, 3,* 255-287.

Bruner, J. (1975). The ontogenesis of speech acts. *Journal of Child Language, 2,* 1-19.

Carter, A.L. (1979). Prespeech meaning relations: An outline of one infant's sensorimotor morpheme development. In P. Fletcher & M. Garman, (Eds.), *Language acquisition* (pp. 71-92). Cambridge: Cambridge University Press.

Clark, E. (1979) Building a vocabulary: Words for objects, actions and relations. In P. Fletcher & M. Garman, (Eds.), *Language acquisition* (pp. 149-160). Cambridge: Cambridge University Press.

Crystal, D. (1986). *Listen to your child.* Middlesex: Penguin Books.

Garman, M. (1979). Early grammatical development. In P. Fletcher & M. Garman, (Eds.), *Language acquisition* (pp. 177-208). Cambridge: Cambridge University Press.

Griffiths, P. (1979). Speech acts and early sentences. In P. Fletcher & M. Garman, (Eds.), *Language acquisition* (pp. 105-120). Cambridge: Cambridge University Press.

McLean, J., & Snyder- McLean, L.A. (1978). *A transactional approach to early language training.* Columbus, Ohio: Charles E. Merrill.

Olswang, L., Stoel Gammon, C. & Coggins, T. (1987). *Assessing linguistic behaviour: Assessing prelinguistic and early linguistic behaviour in developmentally young children.* Seattle: University of Washington Press.

Owens, R.E. (1984). *Language development.* Columbus, Ohio: Bell & Howell.

Prizant, B.M. (1988). *Early intervention: Focus on communication assessment and enhancement.* Workshop presented in Toronto, Ontario.

Reilly, J.S., Zukow, P.G. & Greenfield, P.M. (1984). Facilitating the transition from sensorimotor to linguistic communication during the one-word period. In A. Locke & E. Fischer (Eds.), *Language Development* (pp. 107-131). London: Croom Helm.

Schaffer, H.R. (1984). *The child's entry into a social world.* London: Academic Press.

Smutny, J.F., Veenker, K. & Veenker, S. (1989). *Your gifted child.* New York: Ballantine Books.

Tamir, L. (1984). Language development: New directions. In A. Locke & E. Fischer (Eds.), *Language Development* (pp. 13-20). London: Croom Helm.

Trevarthen, C. Hubley, P. (1978). Secondary intersubjectivity: Confidence, confiding and acts of meaning in the first year. In A. Lock (Ed.), *Action, gesture and symbol: The emergence of language.* (pp. 183-229) New York: Academic Press.

Umiker-Seboek, D.J. (1979). Preschool children's intraconversational narratives. *Journal of Child Language, 6,* 91-109.

Vygotsky, L. (1962). *Thought and language.* Cambridge: MIT Press.

Wetherby, A., Cain, D., Yonclas, D. & Walker, V. (1986). *Intentional communication in the emerging language of normal infants.* Miniseminar presented at the American Speech and Hearing Association Annual Convention, Detroit, Michigan.

Wetherby, A. (1991a). *Profiling communication and symbolic abilities: Assessment and intervention guidelines.* Presentation at Toronto Children's Centre, Toronto, Ontario.

Wetherby, A. (1991b). Profiling pragmatic abilities in the emerging language of young children. In T, M. Gallagher, (Ed.), *Pragmatics of language: Clinical practice issues* (pp. 249-281). San Diego, CA: Singular.

P A R T   2

GET EVERY CHILD IN ON THE ACT – SO ALL THE CHILDREN CAN INTERACT

Teachers in child care settings have to ensure that every child has opportunities to interact with others throughout the day.

Sociable children create these opportunities for themselves. But children who haven't developed the necessary communication and social skills need help so they, too, can get in on the act — and interact!

In Part 2, you will read about getting every child in on the act and helping each one take part in interactions with you and with peers.

Chapter 3, "Let the Child Lead", contains practical information on how to facilitate interactions with even the most withdrawn and hard-to-reach children.

In Chapter 4, "Take Turns Together: Helping Children Become Conversation Partners", you'll discover natural ways of developing children's abilities to take turns during interactions and conversations.

In Chapter 5, "Encourage Interaction in Group Situations: Adapt Your Activities and Routines", we take a look at how to promote interaction and conversation during those busy routines and group activities.

Chapter 6, "Get Yourself Out of the Act: Fostering Peer Interaction", describes the kind of physical environment that encourages peer interaction and what you can do to help socially isolated children become more involved with their peers.

It's not that difficult to get children in on the act. What they need is a stimulating environment, a genuinely interested conversation partner and many opportunities for meaningful communication.

74

CHAPTER 3

Let the Child Lead

A. Letting the Child Lead Enhances Language Learning

Children who initiate frequently and engage their caregivers in social interactions create the ideal conditions for their own language learning — if the caregiver is responsive.

Let's look at what happens when Rhumi, aged 2, picks up a feather from the creative table and shows it to Nina, her teacher.

> **Rhumi:** *Look!* (establishes joint attention)
>
> **Nina:** *Oh, you've got a feather!* (Nina is responsive and provides Rhumi with relevant language input)
>
> **Rhumi:** *Fedder.* (Because Nina's input contains relevant, comprehensible information on the topic that Rhumi has chosen, she listens closely and then imitates the word "feather")
>
> **Nina:** *Yes, it's a feather, from a bird.* (Nina's responses give Rhumi feedback about how well she said "feather" as well as giving her some new information)
>
> **Rhumi:** *Bird? Outside?* (Rhumi requests more information)
>
> **Nina:** *Yes, this feather came from a bird outside.*

Nina is being responsive. She's following Rhumi's lead, providing her with appropriate language input — and Rhumi's language learning is flourishing.

It's doesn't always happen this naturally.

Sometimes teachers change the subject or try to teach too much too quickly, which can turn even the most sociable child off and end the conversation.

Or children don't initiate as easily or as often as Rhumi, so teachers don't have much of a lead to follow. And we've seen the breakdown in communication that results from this: the child contributes too little and the teacher compensates by contributing too much.

When there is a breakdown in communication, it's up to you to open the lines of communication and create opportunities for the child to initiate. You can do this by letting the child take the lead.

Letting Go Of the Lead

Letting the child lead may seem like a simple solution, but it's easier said than done.

The difficulty isn't so much in finding opportunities to let the child lead, even though in child care this is not always possible. For many teachers, the difficulty involves changing long-standing patterns of interaction as well as changing ideas about what a teacher's role really is.

If a teacher is used to playing the role of director, timekeeper or rescuer, it may be hard to let the child select the topic of a conversation or direct an activity.

But teachers who are searching for ways to help children become more confident and interactive will eventually feel more comfortable in the **responsive** role, especially when they see what the child can gain:

• a sense of the power and pleasure of communication

• the desire to initiate in other situations

• many more opportunities to learn language

It's hard to let go of the lead...

...but look at how much fun it can be!

B. Observe, Wait and Listen

Letting the child lead begins with:

Observing

Waiting

Listening

Observing means paying close attention to the child so you can see exactly what she's interested in or what she's trying to tell you.

As adults, we are tuned in to sound. Babies and children who make enough noise will get our attention, whether it's by making sounds, by talking or by crying. But some children, especially those with reluctant or passive conversational styles, haven't figured out the need to use their voice to get attention, nor have they developed the confidence to use it. Their communication may be very subtle, but if you take the time to observe, you'll see what they're saying.

> *Debbie was on the floor with Jerome, a very quiet 11-month-old. She tried to play with him, but felt she was getting nowhere because he just banged his blocks and made no sounds at all.*

Observe closely Debbie! After Jerome banged his blocks, he looked at you three times to see your reaction. That is communication!

Waiting is a powerful tool because it gives the child an opportunity to initiate.

When you wait, you give the child time to initiate or to get involved in an activity. You are, in effect, giving her this message: "You're in control — I know you can communicate, so you decide what you want to do or say. I'll give you all the time you need."

> *Laura was trying to get Margie, a very shy 3-year-old, to talk during a sensory activity with shaving cream. "What colour is it, Margie? How does it feel? What are you going to do with it?" she asked. She got no response.*

Wait and see what Margie does, Laura! That means you have to stop asking questions. When Margie initiates (and she will, when given the chance to play with the shaving cream in her own way), follow her lead.

Waiting not only encourages children to initiate; it also gives them the time to respond to questions and requests.

Studies of adult-child interactions have shown that adults give children approximately one second in which to respond to questions. After one second, the adult repeats or rephrases the question or provides the answer. **One second!** Most children need much longer than one second to process the question and figure out their response. In fact, children who are reflective and think before responding have been shown to do better in school than those who respond quickly and impulsively. So we should be encouraging children to take their time and to think before responding.

If you need to remind yourself to wait, think of the WAIT-AND-SEE WALTZ:

COUNT TO 10

HANDS OFF THE ACTIVITY

NO TALKING

When you don't rush in,
When you observe, listen and wait,
You let the child initiate!

Of course, once the child initiates, you'll respond by doing the TINY TOT TANGO!

Listening means paying close attention to what the child is saying so that you can respond appropriately.

When you listen, you convey the message that what is being said is important — and that's a good reason for a child to continue the conversation.

Active listening involves not interrupting the child or assuming that you understand what she is trying to say before she has finished speaking.

Christine, aged 4 years, was making a collage with cooked, coloured noodles. She picked up a tiny piece of noodle, which was curled into a "U" shape, and glued it on to her paper. Then she showed it to her teacher, Amy, saying "That's a sleigh." Amy, not really listening, said "Yes, and what colour is it?" "Red," answered Christine and turned away.

Listen closely Amy! Christine said something wonderfully imaginative and you missed it. If you'd listened and then said "A sleigh! A tiny sleigh for all the ants at Christmas time!" you would have had a long conversation with her.

It's hard to talk when the "listener" isn't really listening.

It's fun to have conversations when the teacher really listens!

C. Follow the Child's Lead

When you follow the child's lead you pick up on her interest and go with it. No matter how difficult a child may be to interact with, we have to believe that she has something to share, something to say. She just needs the right circumstances. So begin with a positive outlook; instead of focusing on what the child can't or doesn't do, focus on what she could or might do — if you followed her lead.

Instead of being frustrated by what the child can't do...

...focus on what he might be able to do if you followed his lead.

To follow the child's lead, you have to know what her lead is. This can be any sort of initiation: a look, a smile, an offer of a toy, a point toward something, a comment, a question. Even if the initiation isn't directed toward you, it counts as an initiation. Perhaps she starts to play with a toy or begins to explore the fingerpaint. Both these actions are initiations and are signals for you to follow her lead.

Be Face-to-Face

Get down to the child's physical level. Make sure you are face-to-face so that you can look directly into each other's eyes.

For a child, being face-to-face with you adds a special quality to the interaction. It brings you closer physically and emotionally and makes her feel that you're really with her. And when you position yourself face-to-face with a "hard-to-reach" child, she may surprise you by interacting for a long time.

Here are a few ideas for face-to-face positioning:

• You sit on the floor; the child sits on a little chair

• You lie on your stomach; the child (especially an infant) sits on the floor

• You lie on your side with the child sitting on the floor

• You sit on the floor with your knees bent up; a baby can sit on your knees

There's nothing like being face-to-face.

Respond with Interest

The best way to follow a child's lead is to take an interest in what interests the child — and to join in!

> **When you respond to a child's initiation, you can:**
>
> - **Imitate**
> - **Interpret**
> - **Comment**
> - **Join in and play**

Imitate

Follow the child's lead by imitating the child's actions, sounds, facial expressions or words. Do exactly what she does.

Imitation works especially well with children who:

- are at Stages 2 and 3
- are at the functional play stage
- have reluctant or passive conversational styles
- have their own agendas

BaBaBaBa!

BaBaBaBa!

Many teachers have been surprised by "unresponsive" children who become animated and interactive when they are imitated. Although you are likely to get bored with the game long before the child, try not to quit or change the game too soon. What's boring for an adult may be just the beginning of a great time for a child.

Observe, Wait, Listen, then imitate — babies think it's really great!

Interpret

There are two ways of using the technique "interpreting."

Firstly, if you care for young infants who haven't developed the ability to communicate intentionally, then interpret their behaviour as if it were purposeful and intentional.

For example, if a baby looks at a toy, follow her line of vision to see what she's interested in and say, "Oh, you like that bunny!" and give it to her. If she sneezes, you could say, "Oh dear! What a big sneeze!" and if she makes a sound while she's waiting to be taken out of her stroller, you could say, "Yes, I know. You want to get out of your stroller." Even though she doesn't understand what you're saying, you're treating her as if she has intentions, and in time she will come to have them. She'll discover that her behaviour can make things happen and that her sounds, cries, looks and body movements do indeed communicate.

Interpreting is used somewhat differently with a child who can communicate, but not with words (Stage 3). If she is to learn how to send messages **with** words, then she needs you to interpret her messages by "saying it as she would if she could." That way she hears a language model that she can learn from.

Instead of telling the child what you'll do...

...let him hear you "translate" his message, "saying it as he would if he could."

Comment

When you make a comment in response to a child's initiation, she knows that you have received her message and are interested in it. At the same time, you are providing her with information she can learn from.

Respond in a way that shows the child you're interested.

REMEMBER:

• **respond immediately — or you may lose your opportunity**

• **stay with the child's interest — or you may lose the child**

With infants, instead of a longer comment, try a "fun word." Fun words are exactly what the name suggests: words that are fun to listen to. "Boom!" will hold a baby's attention far better than "The blocks fell down," and hearing "Wheeeee!" as she comes down the slide always delights a young child.

Join In and Play

When children are playing, the best way to follow their lead is to join in, especially if you act a bit like a kid!

The way you join in will depend on what kind of play the child is involved in.

When a child is involved in **functional play**, imitation is a wonderful way to start an interaction. Sometimes, after you have imitated her, she will imitate you!

Joining in on a child's **constructive play** may involve playing parallel to her and waiting to see if you're invited to join in. The invitation may be very subtle, like a smile, a change in body position or a look. Or you can join in by asking how you can help with the construction.

When a child is engaged in **dramatic play**, you can join in by pretending along with her. Move in close, change your voice to fit with the character you are playing and have fun. Children enjoy this kind of play with teachers so much that they may never let you go! (Dramatic play will be discussed in more detail in Chapter 9.)

Too much direction usually means less interaction!

When you join in and play, the interaction takes off.

Take the Focus Off Getting the Child to Talk

Many of you work with children who can talk but seldom do. It's frustrating to interact with these children, but the solution is not to **try** to get them to talk by asking questions or by having them imitate words!

Children are very sensitive to such pressure. They know when you are genuinely playing with them and when you are playing with them to get them to talk. **And if your focus is to get a child to talk, you run the risk of losing her.**

The motivating force for communication comes from within, from the desire to connect with others and to feel the satisfaction that results from that connection. Therefore, you have to create environments that encourage children to communicate **because they want to communicate**. Talking because someone else wants you to talk is not communication.

Pressuring a child to talk makes him talk less!

A child who seldom initiates needs time just to play with you, time to establish a connection. She may not talk at all in the beginning. However, as long as you follow her lead and she interacts by looking at you and sharing in the activity, she is experiencing a purpose for communication — social contact. If you are patient and take the focus **off** talking, eventually she **will** talk — because she has something she really wants to say. And the stage is set for language learning.

Surprise! When the pressure is off...

...and the child has something to say, he says it!

D. Watch Turn-taking Take Off

When you **observe, wait, listen** and **follow the child's lead**, you'll have more fun with the children and your interactions with them will last much longer. You'll discover that, quite spontaneously, you and the child are responding in turn to one another. You are, in fact, taking turns.

Turn-taking is a bit like two people taking turns on a see-saw, except that in a conversation, the two people are taking turns sending and receiving messages. The turns may, but need not, involve talking. A turn can be a look, a sound, a point, a sign, a word, a sentence, a story or a combination of these.

Children gain a great deal from the playful, spontaneous interactions they have with you when the turns just keep on going. Not only are they learning language, but they are discovering what it takes to be a conversation partner (and it takes a lot!). Helping children become more effective turn-takers will be expanded on in Chapter 4.

When you observe, wait, listen and follow the child's lead, turn-taking takes off.

E. Set a Limit on Limits

It might seem strange that the topic of setting limits finds its way into a Chapter titled "Let the Child Lead". It might seem that setting limits has little bearing on language development. Yet how limits are set and in which situations they are set can have a significant impact on teacher-child interactions and even on a child's interactions with her peers.

This discussion is not about behaviour that is obviously unsafe, aggressive or disruptive. This is about those behaviours that drive many teachers crazy. It is about the different attitudes teachers bring to limit-setting, based upon their backgrounds, cultures, personalities, moods and day-to-day stresses. It is also about putting children in situations that demand more from them than they are able to give. It is about encouraging natural curiosity, spontaneity and exploration and not expecting too much. It is about letting the child lead whenever possible. It is about creating situations that **prevent** misbehaviour and that provide more opportunities for positive interactions.

> *Let's consider Zoe, who is a 4-year-old with a very loud voice. She is playing with some children in the dramatic play area and, although she doesn't realize it, her voice can be heard right across the room. Joyce, her teacher, tells her to use her "inside" voice, which Zoe does for a few seconds. But she soon gets caught up in the play, and her voice level goes up again. Joyce comes over and says to her: "Zoe, I asked you to use your inside voice and you didn't. So you'll have to go somewhere else, where you can play quietly." Zoe is devastated. She walks around the room, head bowed, not really understanding why she is being punished. She had no idea her voice was so loud. She avoids Joyce and because she feels so unhappy, she doesn't even play with the other children.*

Therein lies the connection between limit-setting and language development: children can become intimidated and disheartened in an environment which imposes too many unnecessary limits. Intimidated and disheartened children initiate less. And teachers who impose unrealistic limits spend a lot of time dealing with behavioural issues and less time having positive interactions with the children. The overall result is a number of dejected children, fewer positive social interactions, and less language learning.

A child may want to initiate, but if she expects a negative response, she won't take the risk.

It All Boils Down to Realistic Expectations

Every day children behave in ways that may appear to be inappropriate. Before you reach this conclusion about a child's behaviour, ask yourself: "Are my expectations realistic?"

It's important to consider the child's age, stage of cognitive and language development, and the overall situation.

Situation 1 — Flour Power!

Akila, aged 4, is playing with flour at the sensory table. She brushes the flour off her hands in an effort to clean them and, as she does, she creates a puff of "smoke." What a surprise! She immediately does it again, but this time she claps her hands together for greater effect. Behold — a nice, big puff of "smoke!" The other children see this and immediately join in, filling the air with huge puffs of "smoke." Sue, the teacher, says "Please stop that. You're getting flour all over the floor."

Instead of putting a stop to the children's play, ask yourself "Are my expectations realistic?"

Sue asked herself: "Are my expectations realistic?"

She wasn't sure; so she gave herself these two tests:

1. The three good reasons test:

"Have I got three good reasons for stopping this activity?"

(This test doesn't apply when the children's safety is involved.)

Sue's reasons for not allowing the flour play —

i) Mess (not a good enough reason)

ii) Noise (not a good enough reason either)

iii) Ummmmm.....(can't think of another reason!)

2. The "Why are they doing this?" test

The children are enjoying the cause-and-effect of clapping their hands and creating a puff of smoke. This is very normal (and desirable) behaviour.

Alternative solution number 1:

- **Allow the behaviour**
  Sue could follow the children's lead by joining in or by commenting on what they are doing.

Sue could follow the children's lead.

Look at that huge puff of smoke!!

Afterwards, Sue could get the children to help clean up the mess on the floor.

You're doing a great job of cleaning up!

Situation 2 — Waiting and waiting... to go outdoors

It's the middle of winter and the toddlers are being helped into their boots and snowsuits for outdoor play. Some of them are all bundled up and ready to go, but they can't go until the others are ready. As they wait, they get hot, sweaty and restless. One child pushes his neighbour and another pulls off his friend's hat. The crying starts and Sylvie, one of the teachers, tells the children to settle down and wait till everyone is ready.

It's hard for children to stay calm when they have to wait and wait to go outside.

Sylvie asked herself: "Are my expectations realistic?"

In this case, no. Toddlers can't be expected to wait patiently, especially when they are so warmly dressed.

Alternative solution number 2:

- **Avoid putting children in situations that they can't cope with**
  Sylvie splits up the groups and those who are dressed first go ahead with another teacher. Not only does this reduce negative interactions, but it increases opportunities for positive interactions. (Adapting routines to encourage interaction will be discussed in more detail in Chapter 5.)

Situation 3 — "But I'm not finished yet!"

Bihnle, aged 4, has been sitting at a table where, for the last fifteen minutes, she has been drawing a very detailed picture. Mark, her teacher, tells her to tidy up because it's circle time. At first, she ignores him, trying hard to finish the last bit of the picture. Mark sees that she's not helping to tidy up, and he tells her to stop what she's doing right away and to go and help the other children. Bihnle bursts into tears, saying "But I'm not finished yet!"

Mark asked himself: "Are my expectations realistic?"

In this case, no. Adults also find it extremely hard to leave something in which they are engrossed. And concentration and persistence are positive qualities — ones that need to be recognized.

Alternative solutions number 3, 4 and 5:

- **Prevent the situation**
  Give the child lots of warning before the transition occurs.

- **Recognize the child's feelings**
  If the child is still not finished when time is up, Mark could say: "It's hard when you want to finish something and you don't have the time."

- **Accommodate the child when possible**
  Mark could let Bihnle join the circle when she has finished her picture. Or he could put the picture in a place where she could come back to it later, perhaps after her nap.

Situation 4 — "You Can't Catch Me!"

Ricardo, aged 2, is walking back to his room from the washroom with Christina, his teacher, and two other children. As they walk through the preschool room to get back to the toddler room, he runs and hides behind a partition. Christina calls him back, but he smiles mischievously and stays put. She tells the preschool teacher that she'll be back for Ricardo and she takes the other two children back to the toddler room. When she comes back for him, she takes his hand and says "I don't like it when you run away from me." Ricardo pulls away and protests loudly.

Christina asked herself: "Are my expectations realistic?"

Well, it seems unrealistic to expect toddlers to do everything they are told. And here Ricardo was obviously initiating a game.

Alternative solution number 6:

• **Avoid a confrontation: Try playful distraction**

Let's picture this another way. Christina hides on the other side of the partition, and says "Where's Ricardo?" Then she jumps out, peering over the partition and squeals "There he is!" Ricardo is delighted. He giggles and crouches low as Christina hides again. The game continues for a few more turns, and then Christina says "I'm going to catch you! You'd better run!" and she pretends to chase him all the way back to their room.

Ricardo and Christina gain a happy interaction and a moment of closeness — and Ricardo still ends up where he's supposed to be.

Situation 5 — All in a Stew

Rashid, aged 18 months, is not very impressed with his lunch. He tries some stew, but he can't seem to sink his teeth into it. He picks up some meat and throws it onto the floor. Heather, his teacher, sees this and says "You're obviously not hungry." She picks him up from behind without warning, takes him to his cot and lays him down. As she walks away, Rashid starts to cry.

Heather asked herself: "Are my expectations realistic?"

Not for an 18-month-old. Rashid still has a lot to learn about table manners! And Heather can use this situation to show him what he **should** do with his food when he doesn't like it.

Alternative solution number 7:

- **Set limits in a positive manner**

    1. Tell the child what he *should* do, rather than what he shouldn't.

        e.g., "Leave your food on your plate, Rashid. See? On the plate."

    2. Give a reason for the limit.

        e.g., "You make a mess when you throw food on the floor. A big mess!"

    3. Reinforce appropriate behaviour

        e.g., "Good, Rashid! Your food is on your plate."

Summary

When teachers let the child lead by observing, waiting, listening and following her lead, they encourage her to initiate and participate actively in interactions. When they imitate the child, interpret her message, make relevant comments and join in and play, interactions are more fun, which ensures more turn-taking and longer interactions. And when teachers set limits only when necessary, interactions in the room remain positive, frequent and enjoyable for everyone.

References

Bondurant, J.L., Romeo, D.J. & Kretschmer, R. (1983). Language behaviour of mothers of children with normal and delayed language. *Language, Speech and Hearing Services in Schools, 14*(4), 233-242.

Bruner, J. S. (1975). The ontogenesis of speech acts. *Journal of Child Language, 2,* 1-19.

Craig, H. K. (1983). Applications of pragmatic language models for intervention. In T. M. Gallagher & C. A. Prutting (Eds.), *Pragmatic Assessment and Intervention Issues in Language* (pp. 101 - 127). San Diego, CA: College-Hill Press.

Deci, E.L. (1980). *The psychology of self-determination.* Lexington, Mass: Lexington Books.

Deci, E.L. & Ryan, R.M. (1985). *Intrinsic motivation and self-determination in human behaviour.* New York: Plenum Press.

Duchan, J.F. (1984). Clinical interactions with autistic children: The role of theory. *Topics in Language Disorders, 4*(4), 62-71.

Fey, M.E. (1986). *Language intervention with young children.* San Diego, CA: College Hill Press.

Girolametto, L. (1986). *Developing dialogue skills of mothers and their developmentally delayed children: An intervention study.* Unpublished doctoral dissertation. University of Toronto, Toronto.

Girolametto, L. (1988). Improving the social-conversational skills of developmentally delayed children: An intervention study. *Journal of Speech and Hearing Disorders, 53,* 156-167.

Harris, J. (1984). Teaching children to develop language: The impossible dream. In D.J. Müller (Ed.), *Remediating children's language: Behavioural and naturalistic approaches* (pp. 231-242). San Diego: College Hill Press.

Hendrick, J. (1984). *The whole child.* St Louis: Times Mirror/Mosby.

Hubbell, R.D. (1977). On facilitating spontaneous talking in young children. *Journal of Speech and Hearing Disorders, 42,* 216-231.

Hubbell, R.D. (1981). *Children's language disorders: An integrated approach.* Englewood Cliffs, NJ: Prentice Hall.

Lieven, E.M. (1984). Interactional style and children's language learning. *Topics in Language Disorders, 4*(4), 15-23

MacDonald, J.D. (1982a). Communication strategies for language intervention. In D.P. McLowry, A.M. Guilford & S.O. Richardson (Eds.), *Infant communication: Development, assessment and intervention* (pp. 83-146). New York: Grune and Stratton.

MacDonald, J.D. (1982b). *Language through conversation: A communication model for language intervention.* Nisonger Center, Ohio State University.

Mahoney, G.J. (1975). Ethological approach to delayed language acquisition. *American Journal of Mental Deficiency, 80* (2), 139-148.

McDonald, L. & Pien, D. (1982). Mother conversational behaviour as a function of interactional intent. *Journal of Child Language, 9,* 337-358.

McLean, J., & Snyder-McLean, L.A. (1978). *A transactional approach to early language training.* Columbus, Ohio: Charles E. Merrill.

Newhoff, M. & Browning, J. (1983). Interactional variation: A view from the language disordered child's world. *Topics in Language Disorders, 4*(1), 49-60.

Prutting, C. (1982). Pragmatics as social competence. *Journal of Speech and Hearing Disorders, 47,* 123-134.

Schaffer, H.R. (1984). *The child's entry into a social world.* London: Academic Press.

Snow, C.E. (1984). Parent-child interaction and the development communicative ability. In R.L. Schiefelbusch & J. Pickar (Eds.), *The acquisition of communicative competence* (pp. 69-107). Baltimore: University Park Press.

Snow, C.E., Midkiff-Borunda, S., Small, A. & Proctor, A. (1984). Therapy as social interaction: Analyzing the contexts for language remediation. *Topics in Language Disorder, 4,*(4), 72-85.

Sugarman, S. (1984). The development of preverbal communication: Its contribution and limits in promoting the development of language. In R.L. Schiefelbusch & J. Pickar (Eds.), *The acquisition of communicative competence* (pp. 23-67). Baltimore: University Park Press.

Wells, G. (1981). *Language through interaction.* New York: Cambridge University Press.

Wells, G. (1986). *The meaning makers: Children learning language and using language to learn.* Portsmouth, New Hampshire: Heinemann.

CHAPTER 4

Take Turns Together:

Helping Children Become Conversation Partners

A. Helping Children Learn the Rules of Conversation

Children must participate in interactions in order to learn to communicate and use language. The more interactions they participate in, the longer these interactions are, and the more information (appropriate to their language level) they hear during the interactions, the more language they will learn. Therefore, we have to help children learn to interact and have conversations, and we begin right after birth!

Think of conversations as a game for two or more players, who may or may not be able to talk. It's quite a complicated game because it has so many rules. And the only way inexperienced players (infants and young children) can learn these rules is by playing the game with a more experienced player (like you). Once they learn the basic rules, their ability to participate in conversations improves, which dramatically increases their opportunities for learning language.

These are some of the rules of the "conversation game":

• initiate interactions, or respond when others initiate

• take a turn at the appropriate time

• give the other person a chance to take a turn

• attend to the speaker

• continue the conversation by taking additional turns on the topic

• send clear messages

• clear up misunderstandings

• stick to the subject (not as easy as it sounds!)

• initiate a new topic, when appropriate

We expect children to have difficulty following all these rules, but adults have difficulty following them too. Think of the adults you know who talk too much or interrupt constantly; they are breaking the rule of giving others a turn. People who don't look at you during a conversation are breaking the rule of attending to the speaker (and making you feel very uncomfortable in the process), and when someone changes the subject abruptly or mumbles, they are breaking the rules of sticking to the subject and sending clear messages.

As the more experienced conversation partner, your task is to create opportunities for the child to interact and to use strategies which help him play the game and learn its rules. This is important for all children, but especially for children who contribute very little to interactions and for children who are language-delayed.

The strategies you use to help children learn the conversation game serve the same function as scaffolds which hold up a building until the supporting structures have been erected. As the construction progresses and the building can support itself, the scaffolds are gradually removed.

> **What a child can do with your support in an interaction, he can't do by himself.**

The scaffolds you use during interactions with infants and young children are called conversational scaffolds. The kinds of scaffolds you use to promote turn-taking depend on the child's ability to converse; you provide more scaffolding to children whose ability to converse is limited and less to children whose conversational ability is more advanced.

You're about to find out what kinds of scaffolds help children take turns (bearing in mind their stage of language development and their conversational ability), and what you can do to help children who have difficulty taking turns and interacting with others.

Teachers can help children become equal partners in conversations.

B. Laying the Foundation for Conversations: Interactions with Children at Stages 1, 2, 3 and 4

At these early stages of communication development, infants and children are learning the basic rules of conversation. Whether they are normally-developing infants or children with developmental or language delays, they need many scaffolds because they can't yet "hold their own" during interactions. You will use fewer and different kinds of scaffolds as the children develop intentional communication (Stage 3) and begin to use words (Stage 4). However, children with language delays may still need many scaffolds beyond these early stages.

Treat Inexperienced Conversation Partners Like Turn-Takers at Stages 1 and 2

Watch a caregiver interacting with a very young infant and you will see how she treats almost anything the baby does as if it were an attempt to communicate. When the baby burps, she says "Oh, what a big burp! Now you feel better!", or when he startles in response to a noise, she says "What was that big noise?"

When you treat an infant's behaviour as if it were intentional, you are establishing patterns of turn-taking long before he has any idea what turn-taking is about. You are giving him a turn, even though he doesn't know it. This starts out as a very one-sided affair because you have to orchestrate the entire interaction and take most of the turns.

Getting a child's attention at this stage is also quite an effort. To get a baby interested in a teddy bear, you might have to:

• call the baby's name a number of times

• make funny faces

• shake the bear in front of him

• touch him with the bear again and again

• say "Here comes the teddy!"

That's a lot of turns for one person! However, as soon as the infant shows some interest by looking at or reaching for the bear, you treat this as his turn. Then, once again, you take a number of turns trying to get another response. It's hard work engaging children who are new to the conversation game.

As the infant develops, you expect more and more from him. By 7 months he has become more interactive and can make babbling sounds, and so you hold out for those kinds of sounds when you're trying to get him to take a turn, no longer accepting burps or coughs.

The principle of "treating inexperienced conversation partners like turn-takers" applies not only to normally-developing infants but also to any child who has not yet developed intentional communication and who has yet to discover his power to affect others.

You **like** my **glasses** don't you ?

Talk to babies as if they can talk to you!

Playing "Peek-a-boo" and "Pat-a-Cake": An Important Part of Learning to Take Turns

Infants and children who are inexperienced turn-takers learn a lot from games like "Peek-a-boo," "Pat-a-Cake" and "Row, Row, Row Your Boat". These games or **social routines** are an important part of infants' earliest social interactions. They are fun and they give babies opportunities to interact just for the pleasure of your company. By playing these games, infants learn the basics of turn-taking and are exposed to simple, repetitive language which helps them learn their first words.

Social routines make turn-taking really easy for infants because:

• the routines have a specific way of being played

• they involve only a few actions, sounds or words

• they are very repetitive

• each person's turn is clearly defined

As you engage the child in these routines and as his ability to interact develops, you will see a marked change in the way he participates and takes turns:

At first — **you** get the interaction going and make it easy for the child to take his turn

Then — with practice, the child becomes familiar with the routine and takes his turn spontaneously

Eventually — he will initiate the routine, and **you** will follow **him!**

Social Routines with Children at Stages 1 and 2: Make it Easy for the Child to Take a Turn

When engaging an infant or child at Stage 1 or 2 in a social routine, your primary aim is to give him a turn or to get him to take one.

Because the child has no idea what he is supposed to do, once again you have to do most of the work. First of all, you have to get the child's attention. So ham it up, be a clown and make sure you're interesting to look at and listen to. (Yes, it's true, you have to be a bit of an entertainer at the beginning!)

You will need to scaffold the interaction by doing the following:

- **Get the child's attention**
  Be face-to-face, call the child's name in an animated way, greet him, and show him the toy you will play with (if there is one).

- **Play the game or sing the song a few times in a very animated way**
  Once the child becomes familiar with how the game is played, he will be better able to take his turn.

- **Pause at an appropriate spot the next time you play the game and look expectantly at the child, as if to say "It's your turn to do something!"**
  For example, if you have been blowing "raspberries" on a baby's stomach, pause before blowing the next one and let him do something to tell you to do it again.

- **Treat any reaction such as a wriggle, a smile, a kick, a burp, a sound or a stare as if the child has taken his turn**
  When the child realizes that by kicking his feet or making a sound he's having a definite effect on your behaviour, he'll do it again — deliberately.

- **Take his turn for him if he doesn't respond; then continue with the game**
  Keep the game going so the child learns how it's played, even if he doesn't take his turn. If he seems uninterested in the game, try a new one.

When you have played the game over and over again and the child comes to know it well, he'll begin to get excited **in anticipation** of the "fun" part. For example, just before the "Weeweewee all the way home" in "This little Piggy went to Market...", he'll wriggle with excitement because he knows the best is about to come.

This baby loves the tickling game.

His wide-open eyes and wriggling body say: "I'm so excited – do it again!"

Social Routines with Children at Stage 3: Provide Plenty of Opportunities for Practice

The child at Stage 3 has become an experienced player of social routines and has developed intentional communication. He can take his turn by performing actions that are part of the game (he'll rock back and forth to tell you to play "Row, Row, Row Your Boat" again) or he'll make sounds at the right time. And if you don't continue the game, he gets very upset.

At this early stage, he has learned the following important rules of conversation:

- attend to the speaker

- take a turn at the appropriate time

- give the other person a chance to take a turn

- continue the conversation by taking additional turns

You can help the child move on to the next stage of turn-taking by:

- ensuring that he has lots of fun when you play these games

- once he knows the game well, changing it slightly so that he learns to take turns in different situations (See "Vary the game's actions or words, especially when the child's interest begins to fade" on page 110.)

- creating new routines (See "Create new routines by treating the child's actions and sounds as initiations" on page 111.)

- providing scaffolds that help him **initiate** the interactions himself (See "Set the stage for **the child** to initiate the routine" on page 112.)

- playing the games frequently to help him figure out how the words are connected to the actions (which will help him learn to say the words)

She knows what to do...

... when YOU play "Peek-a-boo!"

When playing these games with children at Stage 3, remember:

- **Wait expectantly to signal the child that it's his turn**

  Waiting expectantly relates to what you read about in Chapter 3 under "Observe, Wait and Listen". However, in this case you are not simply giving the child time to initiate; you are sending a very strong message that says "I **expect** you to initiate!" When your body language clearly communicates that you expect a child to take another turn, he is far more likely to do so.

  When you stop at that part of the routine where you expect the child to take his turn:

Move in closer

Lean forward

Look animated

Look expectant

Waiting expectantly works wonders!

- **Vary the game's actions or words, especially when the child's interest begins to fade**

  Put the child's name in a song — he'll love it! Or change the words of the song or routine to reflect what he is doing. For example, if he's banging a box, you could sing "Bang, bang, bang the box....." to the tune of "Row, Row, Row Your Boat."

Row, row, row Michael's boat gently **DOWN** the stream......

"Same song, but this one has my name in it, and I love being upside down!"

- **Don't take the child's turn for him if he can take it himself**
  Don't assume that the child needs you to perform the actions in the game. Give him a chance to pull the blanket off your head during "Peek-a-boo" or to make a sound when requesting that you sing a song again. When given a chance to take a turn, he may surprise you.

- **Create new routines by treating the child's actions and sounds as initiations**
  Children will be delighted when you create new routines, especially when these occur in response to their actions or sounds.

Eric likes putting hats on Kara's head...

...so she turned his actions into a new social routine.

Kevin (who is at Stage 3, aged 17 months) is developmentally delayed. He is a passive child who initiates mainly to protest.

Today he is fascinated by a large rubber ball and keeps turning it over and over. Wendy, his teacher, notices him getting very excited when he finds the ball's blow hole. She pokes her finger into the hole, saying animatedly "Look at the hole! Pokey, pokey, pokey!" Kevin is delighted by her "poking" action and by the sound of the word "Pokey." He reaches for her hand and pulls it back toward the hole, telling her to do it again. She repeats "Pokey, pokey, pokey!" And so the "Pokey, pokey" social routine is born.

When you turn a child's sounds or actions into a game by imitating them, you give him the feeling of being an initiator. "Wow, she's following me!" he'll think, and he'll do it again.

- **Set the stage for <u>the child</u> to initiate the routine**
  You can give the child opportunities to initiate well-known routines by getting into position for the game but not starting it. If he is familiar enough with the game, he should do something to get it going. And as soon as he does, PLAY!

Social Routines with Children at Stage 4: Follow the Leader

The child at Stage 4 is no longer a spectator in this game. **He initiates the social routine and takes over your role**, expecting you to respond. For example, he covers his face with his hands to start the "Peek-a-boo" game or holds out his hands and says "Row, Row" to tell you to sing "Row, Row, Row Your Boat." Now that he can initiate a social routine, **he** will run the show, and you will adopt the role he used to play.

This is a great achievement for the child because he realizes the need to be both initiator and responder in interactions. He has learned one of the most important rules of conversation, the rule of "give-and-take", which he will use for the rest of his life.

The child starts the game, and now THE TEACHER is the responder.

Sharing What's on Your Minds: Having Conversations about the Outside World

The development of joint attention, (described in Chapter 2 in the section on Stage 3, under "Social Interaction") changes the way children take turns.

By 10 months, an infant has developed intentional communication and willingly shares his emotions, his intentions, and his interest in the outside world. To do this, he has to establish **joint attention.** In other words, he has to be sure that both you and he are focused on the same thing, and he does this by:

- getting your attention

- letting you know what he's communicating about (establishing the topic of the conversation)

- keeping his own attention both on you and the topic by looking back and forth.

His communication consists of one or more of the following: looking, pointing, showing, giving, making sounds and changing his facial expression. This makes it easy for you to understand and respond to what he's "saying".

Not only does he share his own thoughts and intentions but he is also willing to share yours. When you show him something, he even interrupts his play to look where you are pointing or to watch what you are doing.

Once the child is able to establish joint attention and take turns on a shared topic, his opportunities for learning about the world through his interactions are endless. In addition, your interactions with him become more varied. Before this time, it was hard to play together with toys because he couldn't attend to both you and the toy. Now, you can either join in his play or get him to join in yours. You can show him interesting things, like how a Jack-in-the-Box works or where to put the piece of a puzzle, as long as he's interested. You no longer have to work so hard to get and keep a conversation going.

Jason keeps on looking at his teacher; he's making sure they are both still focused on the same thing, which makes playing and interacting with him so much easier for his teacher.

Helping Children Share What's on Their Minds: Encourage the Development of Joint Attention

Have you ever worked with a child who just didn't seem interested in playing with you, no matter how interesting the toy or how much you followed his lead? A child with a developmental delay may not be able to establish joint attention, even though he is well past the infant stage. In this case, you'll find it frustrating trying to take turns with him during play with toys or objects.

When a child can't establish joint attention, there's no point in trying to help him develop turn-taking skills during object play, because he can't yet focus on both you and the object. Therefore, your aim should be to help him develop joint attention and to give him lots of practice taking turns in situations where he **can** be successful.

You can:

- **Initiate social routines**
- **Create high-interest activities to encourage the development of joint attention**

Initiate Social Routines

Even a child with a significant developmental or language delay will be able to take turns within a suitable social routine. If he is too old for the tried-and-true routines like "Peek-a-boo" and "Pat-a-Cake", create routines to accommodate his age and interests, and make sure you give him a chance to take his turn.

Some of these social routines should involve toys or objects — so that you can encourage the child to shift his eye gaze between you and the toy. Handing an object back and forth is a good social routine for a child at this stage; it helps him develop joint attention because it combines the give-and-take of the object with the need to be aware of the other person. Before handing the object back to the child, move in close and hold on to it for a second; if you're close enough, chances are he'll look at you to request that you give it back to him.

When teachers find ways of interacting with hard-to-reach children, both teacher and child experience the pleasure of social interaction.

The effects of engaging "hard-to-reach" children in social routines can be quite dramatic. When the child becomes an active and willing conversation partner, both he and you will have a different feeling about being together. He will experience the power and pleasure of social interaction and you, no longer feeling frustrated, can begin to view him as a conversation partner with potential.

When you set up an interaction so that the child becomes an active participant, both he and you will have a different feeling about being together.

Create High-interest Activities to Encourage the Development of Joint Attention

To encourage the development of joint attention, use activities or toys that the child really enjoys, and position yourself where it's easy for him to look at you.

> Michael is a 4-year-old with a significant developmental delay, and his teachers find it very difficult to engage him in an interaction. He loves it when they blow bubbles, and he tries to catch the bubbles as they fly away. However, when he wants his teacher to blow more bubbles, he doesn't look at her; he just grabs the bottle or the wand and makes sounds.

Michael's teacher wants to encourage his use of eye contact during this activity, both to request more bubbles and to share his excitement. Therefore, she will need to:

- be face-to-face with Michael to make it easy for him to look at her

- pause after blowing the bubbles to give Michael a chance to take a turn

- get directly in his line of vision when she pauses, and as soon as he gives her even fleeting eye contact, she should say "More bubbles! OK!", and blow more bubbles

- follow Michael's focus of interest by pointing to the bubbles he is trying to catch and commenting on them animatedly, making sure she is close enough for him to make eye contact with her

- draw Michael's attention to one particular bubble (which, for example, may have landed on the ground), in an effort to get him to look at what she's pointing to

- imitate his actions and sounds, which may motivate him to make eye contact with her

You can't teach a child to establish joint attention, but you can scaffold interactions in ways that encourage its development. You have to work hard to make yourself an interesting and animated conversation partner who is tuned in to the child's interests. And you have to make it easy for the child to tune in to you.

Once the child learns to establish joint attention, you can move on to the next stage of turn-taking, which involves sharing what's on your minds and having conversations about the outside world.

Reduce Conversational Overload

Infants and children at the early stages of language development can't understand much of what is said to them. However, their caregivers can help them figure out what words mean, which helps them participate in conversations.

The following strategies reduce conversational overload and are appropriate for infants with normally-developing language skills as well as for older children who have limited receptive language skills.

To reduce conversational overload:

- **Instead of a race, slow down the pace**

- **Adapt your language to help the child understand you**

- **Use questions to keep the child in the conversation**

Instead of a Race, Slow Down the Pace

Teachers in child care often find themselves rushing through routines and activities just to stay on schedule (remember the timekeeper role?). But when you move or speak too quickly or perform an action too many times or too intensely, children become overwhelmed, especially when their receptive language skills are limited. Infants, in particular, are easily overpowered, and when they are they can't take their turn.

So slow down! Pace yourself so the child has time to absorb what you do or say. Then he will take another turn.

Slow down — the baby's getting dizzy!

Adapt Your Language to Help the Child Understand You

Alex has no idea what his teacher is talking about!

When you simplify your language, use exaggerated intonation, emphasize key words and talk about things that are familiar, it is easier for the child to figure out what you mean. In addition, you make yourself interesting to listen to, which increases the likelihood that he will take another turn.

Short and sweet! Now Alex has a better chance of figuring out what his teacher is saying.

Use Questions to Keep the Child in the Conversation

When questions are used appropriately, they really help a child stay in the conversation. But if they are used inappropriately, either because they are too difficult or because they are used to test a child, they can quickly end the conversation.

Questions serve a purpose that's different for children at Stages 2 and 3 from the one for children at Stage 4. When caregivers talk to infants at Stages 2 and 3, they ask **lots** of questions. For example, if you sneezed and an infant looked at you in surprise, quite instinctively you would say "Did I scare you?" rather than "I scared you!" Even though infants at this stage of language development don't understand what we are saying, the question's rising intonation pattern seems to be interesting for them to listen to and helps us keep their attention.

The situation is different for children at Stage 4 because they can understand and say some words. If we ask these children questions that they can understand, we help them take another turn in the conversation. However, the questions should encourage conversation, not test the children's knowledge.

When using questions with children at Stage 4:

• **Ask questions that show your interest and that create anticipation**

The tone of your question conveys your interest and motivates the child to respond.

• **Ask questions that are easy to understand and respond to**
Questions that require a "Yes" or "No" answer and simple "Who?", "What?" and "Where?" questions help keep the conversation going at this stage.

When you know something about the child's life and family, you can use this knowledge to help him participate in conversations — like the teacher in the following example:

Child:	*(pointing to the phone) Da!*
Teacher:	*That's a phone!* (acknowledges his interest) *Do you have a phone at home?* (Yes/No question)
Child:	*Nods enthusiastically*
Teacher:	*Do you talk on the phone?* (Yes/No question)
Child:	*Nana*
Teacher:	*Oh, you talk to Nana.* (confirms child's message) *And do you talk to Jimmy?* (Another family member — Yes/No question)
Child:	*Nods*
Teacher:	*And when you talk to Nana, do you say "Hi! Hi Nana!"?* (Yes/No question)
Child:	*Hi!*
Teacher:	*Yes! You say, "Hi!"* (confirms child's message) *Where's Nana?* (a simple "Where?" question)
Child:	*Go (Gestures "Gone.")*
Teacher:	*Yeah, Nana's gone.* (confirms child's message) *She's at home.* (adds some new information)
	and so on...

By using questions as conversational scaffolds, the teacher has made it possible for a child who can say only a few words to have a real conversation!

- **Ask questions to check that you have understood the child's message**
  When it's hard to understand what the child says, you probably find yourself asking "checking" questions to see if he meant what you think he meant.

- **Ask questions which allow the child to make choices**
  Questions that offer choices are motivating for the child to respond to and are easy to answer because the response is contained in the question.

C. Helping Children Become Equal Partners in Verbal Conversations at Stages 5, 6 and 7

The basic rules of conversation have been learned by the time children become verbal and can talk in sentences, but there's still a long way to go. They still have to learn to "hold their own" in verbal conversations and to exchange information by contributing their thoughts and ideas, just like more mature speakers do.

They must learn to:

- **send clear messages**

- **clear up misunderstandings**
  This includes being aware of whether the listener understands the message or needs more information, and letting the speaker know if something is not understood.

- **begin and end conversations appropriately**

- **contribute to the conversation by adding information which is on the topic and is related to the speaker's previous turn**
  This involves sticking to the subject, which requires the child to attend closely to what the speaker says and to respond appropriately.

- **keep the conversation going for longer periods**

All of this may sound like a huge task, but children learn to do these things as they interact with others during everyday activities and conversations. They learn a lot about conversations from other people's responses to their comments and questions, from the models provided by their conversation partners and, of course, from the way you set up conversations and scaffold them.

Be a Creative Play Partner

It's easier for a child to have verbal conversations with you when the topic of the conversation can be seen by both of you. This places fewer conversational demands on the child because he doesn't have to explain and describe what he is referring to. That's why conversations during play or sensory-creative activities take the pressure off a child who is still learning to have verbal conversations. In addition, the child's turns need not all be verbal or continuous; he may take a turn nonverbally by doing something with the toys or materials, or he may stop interacting for a while as he becomes engrossed in some aspect of the play. All this makes it easier for him to participate in verbal conversations.

Children gain valuable experience by taking turns in verbal conversations during play activities, and you can keep the conversation going even longer by being a creative play partner.

All you need is

- **2 teaspoons of creativity**

- **1 handful of imagination**

- **4 cups of playfulness**

Combine these ingredients and you will have a recipe designed to encourage interaction and extend turn-taking.

Introduce children to activities or ideas that you think will appeal to them. Once you have introduced the activity, give them lots of time and space to get involved with the materials in their own way — and then follow their lead.

Letting the car run down the ramp was fun for a while....

...but making a bridge for the car to go under gives both you and the child more to talk about.

Some other ideas:

- make a wall with blocks for the car to bump into

- change the angle of the ramp and see its effect on the speed of the car

- use different-shaped objects — e.g., balls, blocks, pegs — to see how they go down the ramp

- create a pretend play scene using miniature people and cars

Use Comments and Questions to Continue, Not Control, the Conversation

Remind yourself during interactions and conversations that your aim is to **communicate and exchange information** with the child, to connect and enjoy one another's company. You're not aiming to teach or test him because, as soon as you do, your focus is no longer exchanging information, and chances are that the child will lose his desire to interact.

When you are a responsive conversation partner, your comments and questions communicate your interest to the child, as well as providing him with scaffolds so he can take another turn.

Include Comments in Your Conversations

Comments are often underused by adults in conversations with children who are at Stages 5, 6 and 7. Perhaps we feel that by asking them a question we have a better chance of getting a response. It's true that when children are learning to have conversations, they don't respond as easily to comments as they do to questions. However, they need to learn to respond to comments in order to become effective conversation partners.

Comments can be used to get a conversation started (they act as leading statements), as well as to give children interesting information which they'll want to respond to.

Sarah didn't want to take another turn in response to THIS question.

Include Comments in Your Conversations (continued)

Sarah didn't want to take a turn in response to this instruction either!

This comment captured Sarah's interest, and she WANTED to respond to it!

Avoid Questions That Stop the Conversation

Questions play an important role in keeping the conversation going. But, they can be overused or misused.

- **Testing questions can stop the conversation**
  Questions which test a child's knowledge can stop a conversation dead in its tracks!

Amy wanted her teacher to show an interest in the bears on her sweater, but the teacher wanted to see if Amy could name them ...

...so Amy decided to end the conversation!

> *In order for your questions to keep the conversation going, they have to ask for information that the child is eager to share with you.*

Let's imagine that Joey, a 4-year-old child with a language delay, runs up to show you a white stone he found in the playground. "Look me find!", he exclaims.

If you ask questions like "What colour is it?", "What shape is it?", "How does it feel?" or "What's this called?", you won't capture his excitement and nor will you acknowledge and confirm his interest. Testing questions like these put pressure on the child and keep him from talking about things of real interest to him — such as where he found the stone, whether he's ever seen a stone like this before and what he wants to do with it.

- **Rhetorical questions limit the child's response**
  Questions which don't really require a response are wonderful for infants who react to your tone of voice, but not for preschoolers who have something to say.

  If a 3-year-old shows you a tower he has built and you respond by saying "That's a big tower, isn't it?", it won't do much to keep the conversation going.

- **Complex questions, which are above the child's receptive language level can cause a breakdown in communication**
  Children's understanding of questions develops over time, and questions that begin with "Wh" words are generally more difficult to understand than questions that require a "Yes" or "No" answer.

  Questions that begin with "How?" and "When?" are the most difficult for young children to understand. And when you ask children "Why?" questions, they may say "'Cause," without really understanding what they are being asked.

  You can't avoid asking children questions they don't understand, nor should you try to. However, you should be aware of those questions that will frustrate children or end the conversation because they are inappropriately complex.

  If you ask a child a question such as "How are you getting home today?" and it's obvious that he doesn't understand you, change it to one that he **can** answer, such as, "Who's picking you up today?" or even "Is Mummy picking you up today?" That way, you repair the breakdown in communication.

- **Questions that are too simple or too concrete prevent the conversation from continuing**

The boys would have shared their thoughts if they had been asked the right question.

Ask Questions that Keep the Conversation Going

- **Sincere questions show your interest and encourage the child to respond**

When you ask questions that are sincere (because you really don't know the answer), the child is more likely to respond to them.

• **Ask questions that the child can answer**
Many teachers agree that open-ended questions are the best kind to ask older children. However, sometimes open-ended questions are too broad for the child to answer, and they have to be narrowed down before the child can respond to them. When you do this, you are scaffolding the conversation.

Nicki can't answer this question because it's too open-ended.

When the teacher asks more manageable, focused questions, Nicki can take her turn.

Conversations can go on for a while when the teacher's questions provide the child with scaffolds, as in the following example:

Child: *I saw "Home Alone" last week.*

Teacher: *Really? What was it about?* (open question)

Child: *I dunno.* (question was too broad)

Teacher: *Well, I think it was about a boy whose parents left him alone at home by mistake. And then, do you remember who came to his house?* (question that narrows the focus)

Child: *Bad guys!*

> **Teacher:** *Yeah. Really bad guys! How many were there?* (question that narrows the focus)
>
> **Child:** *Two.*
>
> **Teacher:** *Yeah, there were two of them. But they didn't do anything bad to the little boy, 'cos he was so smart. Remember what he did to the front door handle?* (question that narrows the focus)
>
> **Child:** *Put the heater on it!*
>
> **Teacher:** *Yeah, he was so smart! And then remember what happened to the bad guys when they tried to open the door?* (question that narrows the focus)
>
> **Child:** *They burned their hands!*
>
> **Teacher:** *Yeah, they really hurt their hands!* (comment that invites a response)
>
> **Child:** *And they were screaming!*

These questions helped the child recall what happened, gave him enough cues to give the information that was needed and yet didn't put any unnecessary pressure on him. You can see that the teacher's intention was to help him stay in the conversation, not to test his memory.

- **Combine a question with a comment**
  Often, the best way to keep the conversation going is to:

  First, make a comment which acknowledges the child's message.

  Then, ask a question, which helps the child take another turn.

Let's go back to Joey who found a white stone on page 126.

> **Joey:** *Look me find!*
>
> **You:** *Oh, that's a beautiful stone!* (comment first) *Where did you find it?* (ask a question to help him take another turn)
>
> **Joey:** *Dere (points toward the fence)*
>
> *..... and the conversation continues.*

> *Often, the best way to share a child's interest, curiosity and enjoyment and to keep him involved in the conversation is first to make a comment which acknowledges his interest, and then to ask a question which helps him take another turn.*

- **Interesting questions that have no "right" answer stimulate children's creative thinking**

We don't ask children enough questions that stimulate creative thinking and problem-solving.

Too many questions asked of children are **fact questions** which have only one right answer. These questions test the child's memory, ability to label or simply to provide the "right" answer. Questions such as "What do we call a person who delivers mail?" or "Who remembers what we put in the playdough?" don't even begin to tap children's abilities to think creatively.

Figuring-out questions require more thought and reasoning on the child's part than fact questions. Questions such as, "In what way are balls the same as oranges?" involve some analysis on the child's part and some understanding of higher-level concepts, but they still require a closed-end, "right" answer.

Creative questions encourage children to be creative because there are no right or wrong answers; children are free to come up with their own original, imaginative ideas. Questions such as "What could we do about it?" "What might happen if...?" "Suppose that..." or "What would you do if that were you?" challenge the child to think of more than one answer and encourage the kind of thinking that develops creativity and problem-solving.

Creative questions get creative answers!

(In Chapter 8, there is a section titled "Provide Support to the Storyteller", which contains information on the kind of questions that help children provide necessary information when they tell stories.)

Requests for Clarification: Encourage Children to Let You Know When They Don't Understand You

One of the rules of the conversation game is that the listener is expected to let the speaker know when his or her message is unclear. Early on in their conversational lives, children learn to **request clarification** from the speaker, getting him or her to repeat or rephrase a comment or question that the child has not heard properly or understood. Very young children may look at you quizzically when they don't understand you, or they may say "Huh?" or "What?" And when they do, you repeat your message in a way that they can understand.

Some children with language delays don't request clarification. They may not realize that they don't understand what has been said and even if they do, they may do nothing about it. As a result, they are at a serious disadvantage in all aspects of learning, including language learning. In later years, children who don't request clarification can end up confused, bored, frustrated and passive in school, and this pattern may continue unless they are taught to request clarification.

You can help young children learn to request clarification by modelling such a request in a small group.

> *Roberto is a language-delayed 3-year-old whose language development is at Stage 5. He has a reluctant conversational style and doesn't request clarification when he can't understand what is said to him. It is snack time, and he is sitting in a group with three other children and their teacher, Lenore.*
>
> *Sandy, aged 2½, shows his cracker to Lenore and says something which no one can understand. Lenore looks at the children, making sure she has a confused look on her face. She gestures "I don't know" with her hands up in the air as she says "I didn't understand what Sandy said. Roberto, let's ask Sandy 'What?'" (She leans forward) "Sandy, what?" Sandy (with a bit of luck) repeats what he said, and then Lenore says "Oh! Your cracker is broken. See Roberto, Sandy's cracker is broken!"*

This modelling process can begin when children are at Stage 5, and it should continue to be used with older children who have more advanced language skills. For these children, you should model more socially appropriate questions such as "What did you say?" or "What do you mean?"

When children don't request clarification, they place total responsibility for a successful conversation on their partner, which causes problems in both adult-child and child-child interactions. This passive behaviour is often seen in children with reluctant or passive conversational styles, and it may have lifelong consequences.

Sticking to the Subject: A Sticky Problem

Have you ever had conversations with a child who takes turns off the topic and not been sure what to do about it? Well, children need to know that they have strayed off topic, and you can help them realize that they have broken a conversational rule by redirecting them back to the original topic.

Shari is talking to Thomas, aged 4, about his cousin's new puppy.

Thomas: *The puppy bited me.*

Shari: *Where did he bite you?*

Thomas: *My Dad took me home.*

Shari: *Where did the puppy bite you? Can you show me where?* (Redirects the topic)

Thomas: *Here. (shows his arm)*

Shari: *On your arm. Wow, I can see the teeth marks. And your Dad took you home after the dog bit you?* (acknowledges the child's statement once he answers the original question)

Thomas: *Yeah, I was crying.*

Shari: *It must have really hurt. Is it better now?*

If the child says something that is totally unrelated to the topic, don't just go along with it; let him know that he's done something to cause a breakdown in communication. Look confused and tell him that you don't understand or that you were talking about something else — he can only learn to play the conversation game when someone lets him know the rules.

Help Children Learn to Give and Take Turns in a Group, Especially Those Children Who Don't Give Anyone Else a Turn!

When you interact with children in small groups, the turn-taking is often unequal. There is often a child who dominates the conversation, talking a lot, interrupting others and answering for them; and there is often another child who seems unable to find his way into the conversation.

You can help children understand what kind of turn-taking behaviour is and is not appropriate in a group situation — by spelling it out for them. Tell them whose turn it is, that they must wait for their turn, and that they can't butt in or answer for another child.

Maya, a junior kindergarten teacher, is sitting with a group of five 4-year-olds at the snack table.

Tom:	*Maya, I've got a new racing car at home. It goes so fast!*
Brett:	*(Interrupting) My Dad bought me...*
Maya:	*Brett, (holds up her hand as if to say "Stop") Tom was talking, so it's his turn. Tom, tell me about your new car.*
Tom:	*It goes so fast. It goes vrooom! Like that.*
Maya:	*Wow! It sounds like it's faster than a racing car. Does it look like a real racing car?*
Tom:	*Yeah, it is like a real one.*
Maya:	*You're lucky, Tom. (Turns to Brett) Okay, Brett, now it's your turn.*
Brett:	*My Dad bought me a truck wif big wheels, and a man can sit inside.*
Maya:	*Does it make a noise when you drive it?*
Brett:	*Yeah, a big noise, and you know what else?*
Maya:	*What?*
Brett:	*I saw a real truck like that at a farm...... (keeps talking for a while)*
Maya:	*Brett, it's time to give someone else a turn to talk. (Turns to a quiet child) Shannon, do you ever play with trucks or cars at home?*
Shannon:	*(Looks at teacher shyly)*
Brett:	*She don't play wif trucks. I got even more trucks....*
Maya:	*Brett, (holds up her hand as if to say "Stop") I asked Shannon a question, so it's her turn to talk.*

Helping children learn the rules for group conversations may seem like directing traffic, but it can go a long way to helping them understand how group conversations work.

D. Making Time for One-to-One Interactions

From time to time, children need your undivided attention. Although it's not easy, it is possible to sneak some one-to-one interactions into your busy day.

Take Turns on the Run

Every minute counts! A brief conversation is better than no conversation at all.

When <u>a child</u> initiates an interaction:

• Stop what you are doing for a moment; and

• Get down to his level; and

• Respond warmly to him

When <u>you</u> initiate an interaction:

• Say something inviting — e.g., "You made a really big tower!"; and

• Wait for a response; and

• Take a few turns with the child; and then

• Let the child know you have to leave before you go.

Instead of rushing off.....

Those are nice shoes!

....stop and chat for a minute.

You've got beautiful new shoes!

Make the Most of the Quiet Times

It may be early morning

Or afternoon when it's late,

But quiet times are best times

To communicate

Make the most of those quiet times when you have only three or four children in your room. Rather than use these times to tidy up or to prepare materials, spend some time with the children who really need one-to-one interactions.

Going home late isn't so bad if I get all this attention!

Let Them Help You

All children love to help. Cleaning paintbrushes, wiping dirty tables or handing out cups at snack time are all special treats for children. So instead of rushing through some of your chores, let one or two children help you. There's so much to talk about when you work together.

It's a real treat for a child to help with chores.

Summary

Children learn to be conversation partners by taking part in many, many interactions with supportive adults. To help children become conversation partners teachers need to scaffold conversations in ways that make it easy for the children to take their turn. Infants and children with significant language delays require a great deal of scaffolding, whereas children whose conversational ability is more advanced require less scaffolding. Scaffolds include playing social routines with the child and pausing to indicate that he should take his turn, using questions and comments appropriately, redirecting the child who strays off topic and spelling out the rules for taking turns in a group situation. Teachers can also enhance children's conversational skills by making time for one-to-one interactions.

References

Bates, E., Camaioni, L. & Volterra, V. (1979). The acquisition of performatives prior to speech. In E. Ochs & B. B. Schieffelin (Eds.), *Developmental pragmatics* (pp. 111-129). New York: Academic Press.

Berko Gleason, J. (1989). *The development of language.* Columbus, Ohio: Merrill.

Bruner, J.S. (1975). The ontogenesis of speech acts. *Journal of Child Language, 2,* 1-19.

Bruner, J.S. (1983). *Child's talk: Learning to use language.* New York: Norton.

Cazden, C.B. (1983). Adult assistance to language development: Scaffolds, models, and direct instruction. In R.P. Parker and F.R. Davis (Eds.), *Developing literacy* (pp. 3-18). International Reading Association.

Cross, T.G. (1984). Habilitating the language-impaired child: Ideas from studies of parent-child interaction. *Topics in Language Disorders, 4*(4), 1-14.

Donahue, M. (1985). Communicative style in learning disabled children: Some implications for classroom discourse. In D. N. Ripich & F. M. Spinelli (Eds.), *School discourse problems* (pp 97-124). San Diego: College Hill Press.

Foster, S. (1985). The development of discourse topic skills by infants and young children. *Topics in Language Disorders, 5* (2), 31-45.

Girolametto, L. (1986). *Developing dialogue skills of mothers and their developmentally delayed children: An intervention study.* Unpublished doctoral dissertation. University of Toronto, Toronto.

Girolametto, L. (1988). Improving the social-conversational skills of developmentally delayed children: An intervention study. *Journal of Speech and Hearing Disorders, 53,* 156-167.

Hendrick, J. (1984). *The whole child.* St Louis: Times Mirror/Mosby.

Kaye, K. & Charney, R. (1980). How mothers maintain "dialogue" with two-year-olds. In D. Olson (Ed.), *The social foundations of language and thought* (pp.211-230). New York: Norton.

Lucariello, J. (1990). Freeing talk from the here-and-now: The role of event knowledge and maternal scaffolds. *Topics in Language Disorders, 10*(3), 14-29.

MacDonald, J.D. (1989). *Becoming partners with children: From play to conversation.* San Antonio, Texas: Special Press.

MacDonald, J.D. & Gillette, Y. (1984). Conversational engineering: A pragmatic approach to early social competence. *Seminars in Speech and Language, 5,* 171-184.

McDonald, L. & Pien, D. (1982). Mother conversational behaviour as a function of interactional intent. *Journal of Child Language, 9,* 337-358.

Mirenda, P.L. & Donnellan, A.M. (1986) Effects of adult interaction style on conversational behaviour in students with severe communication problems. *Language, Speech and Hearing Services in Schools, 17,* 126-141.

Newson, J. (1978). Dialogue and development. In A. Lock (Ed.), *Action, gesture and symbol: The emergence of language* (pp. 31-42). London: Academic Press.

Owens, R.E. (1984). *Language development.* Columbus, Ohio: Bell & Howell.

Prizant, B.M. (1988). *Early intervention: Focus on communication assessment and enhancement.* Workshop presented in Toronto, Ontario.

Ratner, N. & Bruner, J. (1978). Games, social exchange and the acquisition of language. *Journal of Child Language, 5,* 391-401.

Sachs, J. (1984). Children's play and communicative development. In R.L. Schiefelbusch & J. Pickar (Eds.), *The acquisition of communicative competence* (pp. 109-140). Baltimore, MD: University Park Press.

Spinelli, F.M. & Ripich, D.N. (1985). Discourse and education. In D. N. Ripich & F. M. Spinelli (Eds.), *School discourse problems* (pp 3-10). San Diego: College Hill Press.

Terrel, B.Y. (1985). Learning the rules of the game: Discourse skills in early childhood. In D. N. Ripich & F. M. Spinelli (Eds.), *School discourse problems* (pp 13-27). San Diego: College Hill Press.

Trevarthen, C. & Hubley, P. (1978). Secondary intersubjectivity: Confidence, confiding and acts of meaning in the first year. In A. Lock (Ed.), *Action, gesture and symbol: The emergence of language* (pp. 183-229). London: Academic Press.

Verbey, M. (1992). *Improving joint engagement in parent-child interaction: Reanalysis of an intervention study.* Unpublished master's thesis, University of Toronto, Ontario.

Warr-Leeper, G. (1992). *General suggestions for improving language.* Presentation at Clinical Symposium on "Current Approaches to the Management of Child Language Disorders" University of Western Ontario, London, Ontario.

Wells, G. (1981). *Learning through interaction: The study of language development.* New York: Cambridge University Press.

Wells, G. (1986). *The meaning makers: Children learning language and using language to learn.* Portsmouth, New Hampshire: Heinemann.

C H A P T E R   5

Encourage Interaction in Group Situations: Adapt Your Activities and Routines

A. Interact with Every Child in the Group: You Can if You Scan

Sometimes a teacher doesn't realize that a child is being left out.

Some children don't have the confidence or the social skills to compete for your attention in a group. Therefore, they need you to help them get in on the act.

Difficult as it is to interact with all the children, you **CAN** if you **SCAN** and if you take the time to focus on each child in the group.

The letters of the word SCAN can help you put this technique into practice:

Small	**C**arefully	**A**dapt	**N**otice
groups are best	observe each child throughout the activity	your response to each child's focus	which children are demanding your attention

Small groups are best

Interactions are more relaxed and children get more attention when the group is small. Limit, if possible, the group size to three or four children.

Carefully observe each child throughout the activity

Scan the group on and off during the activity and observe each child's focus.

Adapt your response to each child's focus

Let's say that you and four preschoolers are playing "Restaurant". Two children are "serving" food, one is pretending to cook it and the other is at the cash register, pretending to be the cashier. Once you have observed what each child's focus is, it's easy to follow her lead.

Notice which children are demanding your attention

Be aware how easy it is to ignore quiet children when there are sociable children around. Make a point of observing the less interactive children so you can pay more attention to them and follow their lead.

REMEMBER

Because it's natural to interact more with children who are positioned directly across from you, position yourself opposite the least interactive children. Then it's easy for you to make eye contact with them and vice versa. You will also be able to pick up their initiations, which might be subtle — e.g., the child might glance at you or lean over slightly to see what someone is doing. If you seat yourself next to a less interactive child, these subtle initiations are likely to be missed.

When you SCAN, you tune in to each child's focus and follow her lead.

Play with me!

Play with me too!

And now me!

Scan the Entire Room

When you scan the whole room, you may notice children who are not engaged in activities or interactions. These children would be categorized as "unoccupied" or "onlookers" (see section on "Observing Peers at Play" in Chapter 1), and they need help getting in on the act!

All the other children are busy playing, but Patrice is unoccupied.

The teacher scans the room and notices that Patrice is sitting alone, doing nothing; so she invites her to join in and play.

Patrice, come play with the cars.

Wheee! There goes your car!

Now Patrice is in on the act!

B. Encourage Exploration and Conversation during Sensory-Creative Activities

Sensory-creative activities offer children unique opportunities to explore, experiment and create in an environment where it's okay to make a mess! At times teachers leave the children alone to explore the materials, particularly children who have reached preschool age. At other times, teachers sit at the table and capitalize on the children's desire to share their discoveries, sensations and creations.

The fun isn't just in exploring, but in sharing the pudding and the experience with you.

Setting up Sensory-Creative Activities

By following a few simple guidelines, you can set the stage for the children to explore and create during sensory-creative activities, as well as to **share** the fun and wonder of their experiences.

2. Let the children help prepare the materials

The children are mixing the paint powder and water by themselves, something they love to do.

1. No more than four children

The group is small so that the teacher can interact with each child.

3. Have your own spot

The teacher makes it easy for the children to interact with her by sitting beside them in her own spot (preferably at their eye level).

4. Provide materials that are age-appropriate and open-ended

The teacher considers the children's ages and stages of development when deciding what kinds of activities to offer them.

5. Have more than enough materials for each child

Each child has her own container or supply of materials, and enough for her to really get "stuck in."

6. Be well-prepared

The teacher has all the materials ready, with a pail beside her for clean-ups. She has no need to leave the table.

The Teacher's Role Really Makes a Difference

There's so much children can learn and discover during sensory-creative activities when you play the **Responsive Teacher Role**.

The responsive teacher:

- provides no props the first time new material is presented, so the children can explore it thoroughly

- by not always supplying props, she encourages children of preschool and kindergarten age to use their imaginations. For example, she knows that children will make many imaginative creations out of playdough if cookie cutters are not supplied.

- gives the children time to explore the materials and encourages them to do this in their own way

- uses her own materials, so she never has to take materials from a child

- when providing props for older children, provides open-ended ones, such as sticks, stones and strips of cardboard, which encourage creative and imaginative use of the materials

- responds to children's initiations, neither talking too much nor asking unnecessary questions such as "What are you making?" or "What is that?" (they may not know!)

When children are given opportunities to explore and create,
each child will do it in a different way.

Wait, and Observe Each Child's Focus

At the beginning of the activity, wait, wait, wait and give the children lots of time to get involved with the materials. This is the moment to sit silently and observe what they do, or to play silently with your own materials.

Follow The Children's Lead and Join in

When a child initiates during a sensory-creative activity, there are a number of ways in which you can respond:

Look, it's dripping!

Yes, it **PLOPS** every time it hits the tray !!!

MAKE A COMMENT that shows your interest.

IMITATE the children, but use your own materials.

JOIN IN on the children's MAKE-BELIEVE.

When you let the children lead the way, interactions during sensory-creative activities are lots of fun and can last a very long time.

C. Adapt Daily Routines to Make Time for Conversation

"Get dressed quickly so we can go outside."

"Hurry and eat your snack so we can go and play."

"Not so much talking! Wash you hands and go and eat."

Does this sound familiar? Do you spend much of your time during routines trying to keep everyone on task?

No one will argue that, at times, daily routines can challenge the patience of the most patient teacher. On the days when there's a lot of crying (the children's, not yours) and when nothing is going according to plan, it may seem best to get the routine over with as quickly as possible. On days like these, you may be right!

Although routines can be stressful both for you and the children, they can promote positive relationships and language learning. Every routine has the potential for some interaction, no matter how brief. With some creative planning and allowance for flexibility, routines can be adapted so that they are more relaxing and interactive for everyone.

Four Factors that Make or Break Interactions during Routines

> **The following four factors will each affect how much interaction occurs during a daily routine:**
>
> **1. The number of teachers and children**
>
> **2. The physical environment**
>
> **3. The timing and pacing of the routine**
>
> **4. The role the teacher plays**

1. The Number of Teachers and Children

During a routine, teachers become stressed and children become restless and rowdy when there are too many of them and too few of you to help them. In all the noise and confusion, there are few opportunities for positive interactions.

There has to be a better way to get children ready for outdoor play.

Consider the following solutions:

- **Have all teachers available to help**
  Many directors of child care centres organize staff schedules so that all teachers are available during the busy routines of the day.

- **Split the group up**
  Smaller groups make for less noise and confusion and make "turns-on-the run" possible. When dressing children for outdoor play in the winter, it helps for one teacher to go ahead with the group which is ready first.

Cut down on waiting time;
take out the children who are ready.

- **Stagger the routine**

  If the toddlers don't all go to the bathroom at the same time and the infants don't all eat at 11:30 a.m., you'll have fewer children to contend with and many more opportunities for interaction.

To make time for interaction,
try to stagger routines.

2. The Physical Environment

A well-designed physical environment will increase opportunities for interaction.

Consider these aspects of your environment:

- **The place where the routine is conducted**
Sometimes a lack of space makes interaction difficult. For example, if all the toddlers are putting on their snowsuits in a small area, they are more likely to push and shove one another than in an area with more space.

- **The equipment**
The equipment you use can make or break a routine. For example, there is likely to be less interaction at one large lunch table with 10 children and two teachers than at two smaller tables each with five children and one teacher.

- **How you set up the environment**
Let's take a look at mealtimes again. Ideally, teachers should plan and prepare everything in advance so that they can sit and interact with the children.

One child care centre invented the "runner" system to deal with the problem of teachers constantly leaving the table to get food or drinks for the children. This system involves one teacher being the "runner" and being responsible for bringing the food (and anything else) to each table, where it is served by another teacher. It helps to have a small cart or table for the serving bowls and supplies beside each table so that the teacher can serve the food from her seat. Except for the "runner," all teachers sit and interact with the children in a relaxed atmosphere.

Lack of preparation and a line of high chairs is a recipe for disaster!

| **Solution 1** | *There will be less crying and more interaction when the babies sit at the table.* |

| **Solution 2** | *Semi-circles, a table for supplies beside the teacher's chair and plenty of preparation make all the difference. Now there are opportunities for interaction.* |

3. The Timing and Pacing of the Routine

Consider these aspects of timing and pacing routines:

- **The time of day**
  There are busy times of day, and then there are **busy, busy** times of day! Some routines have to involve **all** the children at the same time, but others can be staggered. For example, toddlers can have bathroom routine as they arrive in the morning.

- **The pacing and amount of time taken to complete the routine**
  Hurried routines produce harassed teachers and frustrated children. And if routines are not well-planned, the children spend too much time waiting for the rest of the group. The goal, therefore, is to have well-organized routines which allow for a slower pace and more interaction.

Particularly with infants, routines like diaper-changing and feeding provide nurturing one-to-one interactions; they should not be rushed.

In the long run, a well-organized routine which allows for interaction won't take any longer than a rushed, poorly-planned routine. And if some waiting on the children's part is unavoidable, teachers should be prepared to keep them occupied with stories, songs or other activities.

4. The Role the Teacher Plays

In the end, the success of a routine depends on you and your responsiveness to the children. If you take the time to observe and listen to them, to respond to their initiations and to pay some attention to each child, your routines won't be routine — they will be some of the best times of the day.

Instead of talking to the other teachers...

...sit with the children and have a conversation.

Some Shared Thoughts on the Dreaded "Dressing-for-Outdoor-Play" Routine

Many teachers say that getting children dressed for outdoor play on cold, wintry days is the most difficult of all the daily routines. While teachers and children who live in warm climates have been playing in the sun, these teachers have been developing some creative solutions to make the routine more organized, more interactive and less traumatic.

About improving the interaction...

"When helping children get dressed, we remind ourselves of the importance of interacting with each child by thinking of the beginning, middle and end of the conversation. The beginning involves responding to the child's request for help, offering our help or just seeing how she is doing. The middle involves either responding to her initiation or talking to her about something we think will interest her. The end involves "closing" the conversation by saying something like, 'You're all ready to go and play. Now I'm going to help Simon.' It's important to do all three."

"We realized that we were often dressing children from behind and were not even looking at the child we were helping! Even when we **were** in front of the child, we kept on looking around the room, talking to other children and ignoring the child we were with. Now we dress the child face-to-face and make an effort to interact as much as possible with the child we are helping."

About preventing the children from getting hot and bothered...

"We leave jackets and hats off till everyone has their snowpants, boots and scarves on. Only then do we put on jackets and hats — that way the children don't get so terribly hot and irritable."

"There are some children, especially in the infant and toddler rooms, who just hate to be dressed up in their snowsuits, and so we leave them till last. We let them look at a book or watch the others getting ready until we can help them. Then we dress them, trying to keep them calm by talking to them. As soon as these children are ready, we head out — fast!"

About taking the time to encourage self-help skills...

"When it gets cold enough to wear snowpants outside, we spend some time in small groups showing the toddlers how to put on their snowpants. This is done at the end of playtime, while some of the children are still playing. In this way, we can spend time with those children who need to be guided through each step of putting on their snowpants. It really pays off later!"

Summary

Working with groups of children presents teachers with the challenge of interacting with every child on and off throughout every day. There are many ways for teachers to provide children with the attention and interaction they need in a group situation. The technique of scanning enables teachers to monitor all the children in the group and to pay attention to each one. In addition, interactions during daily routines can be increased by adapting the following: the ratio of teachers to children, the physical environment, the timing and pacing of the routine and the role the teacher plays. There are many ways for creative teachers to make routines less stressful, less rushed and, as a result, more interactive.

References

Day, D. (1983). *Early childhood education: A human ecological approach.* Scott, Foresman.

Gonzalez-Mena, J. (1986). Toddlers: What to expect. *Young Children, November,* 47-51.

Hendrick, J. (1984). *The whole child.* St Louis: Times Mirror/Mosby.

Striker, S. (1986). *Please touch.* New York: Simon and Schuster.

Yardley, A. (1973). *Young children thinking.* London: Evans Brothers.

C H A P T E R   6

Get Yourself Out of the Act: Fostering Peer Interaction

A. Children Who are Socially Isolated Can't Go It Alone

Children need to take part in playful peer interactions.

In order to become well-adjusted human beings, children need to interact with other children; even at the toddler stage, interactions with caregivers can't replace interactions with peers.

By 3 years of age, children in group settings interact more with peers than with teachers — or they should (see Chapter 1 for more information on the development of peer interactions). Because a lack of peer interactions can have a negative effect on a child's social, intellectual and language development, we should be very concerned about children aged 3 or older who are ignored or rejected by their peers.

Peer interactions at the preschool stage require many high level skills, one of which is well-developed verbal conversational ability. Children have to be able to initiate interactions, respond when others initiate, send clear messages, continue the conversation, clear up misunderstandings and stick to the subject (see Chapter 4 for information on how children learn the rules of conversation). Children who seldom initiate or respond during peer interactions are breaking the basic rules of conversation and are likely to end up being ignored by their peers.

However, it's not enough for children to know the rules of conversation; they have to know when and how to use them. For example, a child may be able to initiate peer interactions, but if he does this by dumping a truck on top of another child's block construction, saying "Let's play with my truck!", he's not going to get a positive response!

When we engage in social interactions, we constantly analyze the situation, figure out what kind of behaviour is appropriate to that situation and make the necessary adjustments as the conversation continues. This is a complex process which takes years to develop and refine. Children have to do this during interactions with their peers, and they have to learn to consider the situation as a whole as well as the other person's needs, feelings and point of view. For example, if a 4- or 5-year-old child wants to join a group of children, he might start out by asking if he can play. If he is refused permission, he might ask again in a more pleading tone or, depending on the situation, he might state aggressively that he has a right to join in or even suggest a role for himself. If he is still refused, he might argue or stay close to the group and try to edge his way in. This kind of ongoing behavioural adjustment enables children to find solutions to problems with peers and to keep interactions going.

When a preschool child doesn't have the necessary cognitive and language skills to analyze a social situation, his interactive behaviour will often be inappropriate. This will result in rejection by peers, who may think of his behaviour as "mean" or "weird."

Until children learn to analyze social situations and adjust their behaviour accordingly, there is an awful lot of conflict during peer interactions.

Children who are socially isolated can't learn complex social skills simply from being with sociable children. They need support, guidance and behind-the-scenes engineering. And in many cases, some specific social skills will have to be taught to them.

This chapter, which is aimed primarily at children 3 years and older, contains information on how to set up environments which facilitate peer interaction and describes ways to help children gain entry into peer groups and take part in interactions.

To help children learn specific social skills, you will need additional information beyond the scope of this book. There are a number of programs and approaches designed to improve children's social skills. Some use peers as models, tutors or social reinforcers, and some teach children a problem-solving approach to peer interactions. Since we know that social skills are unlikely to improve without help, it is a good idea to investigate the programs that are available in your community.

B. The Three Kinds of Peer Groups

Three kinds of peer groups can be identified in preschool settings, and children benefit from being involved in each one. Therefore, your efforts at promoting peer interactions should aim at involving children in all three.

a) Pairs

Because it is less demanding to interact with one child than with a number of children, preschoolers spend much of their time in pairs. Paired interactions are often brief, but some twosomes become "best friends" and are seldom seen apart.

b) Casual Large Groups

Casual groups form at activity centres where children come and go as they wish — for example, at the water, sand or playdough table. Associative play is common in these groups, and interactions may not last very long. However, casual groups offer children the stimulation of interacting with peers in play situations which are relatively undemanding.

c) Cooperative Groups

Cooperative groups are the most highly organized, stable and socially-demanding groups. They consist of a small number of children, one of whom is the leader, which is particularly obvious during sociodramatic play. Because participation in cooperative groups is dependent on a child's language and social skills, these groups are usually composed of children who are highly verbal and imaginative.

Cooperative groups attract children who are highly imaginative and verbal.

C. Create an Environment that Encourages Peer Interaction

Child care environments are not all created equal. Some encourage peer interaction; others don't — because of the way they are designed and equipped.

Open Space May Be Too Much of a Good Thing

The way you make use of space in your classroom affects group interaction. Classrooms that have shelves and tables lined up against the walls and a large open space in their centre discourage peer interaction.

Too much open space:

- encourages running, fighting and noisemaking

- discourages intimate peer interactions

- discourages quiet activities such as book reading

- results in teachers spending too much time setting limits

Rooms with large open spaces encourage noisy, boisterous behaviour and discourage extended, intimate peer interactions.

Make the Best Use of Space

- **Create well-defined play areas by breaking up large, open spaces with low partitions and furniture**

Classroom environments encourage peer interaction (pairs and cooperative groups, in particular) when they have a variety of well-defined play areas, which offer some privacy. Such environments bring children closer together physically and socially, and reduce distractions.

If you have a room with a large open space in its centre, consider closing it up to increase peer interaction. Use shelving, couches, tables or low partitions to break up the room. The house centre will then feel more like a house, and constructions in the block centre will be protected. The more privacy the area needs, the more enclosed sides it should have.

Activity centres or play areas need not all be at the edge of the room; well-defined areas in the **centre** will reduce open space and encourage group interaction. In addition, your partitions need not all be at right angles; placing furniture or partitions diagonally creates interesting spaces that attract children.

Use low partitions so that the children inside the play area can see the rest of the room, and the children outside can see what each play area contains. When you have made the changes, crouch down to see how it looks from a child's perspective!

- **Not too close, please**

Close up large areas, but not too much! Small areas lead to crowding, which discourages group interaction. The amount of available space in each area should allow for free movement, without children bumping into one another. Block areas, for example, need a large space, as does the dramatic play area.

It is especially important to make an area large enough to accommodate children who engage in solitary or parallel play. This set-up provides these children with space to play, as well as with opportunities to work their way into the group.

- **Create private spaces**

  Sometimes children need to get away from it all — to rest, to think, to dream, to relax for a while (sounds appealing doesn't it?). At home, they can often do this, but in child care settings, it's not that easy. Perhaps giving children a private place to go to will give them an opportunity to re-energize and come back to the group ready to play.

  Private spaces can be anywhere — behind a partition or a couch, under a makeshift tent or, best of all, in a large appliance box!

- **Keep quiet and noisy areas separate**

  The music area, for example, shouldn't be close to the book centre because the noise will discourage children from going to look at books. Book centres encourage interaction when they have comfortable seats for more than one child and when they are sheltered and quiet.

- **Put areas that complement one another close together**

  Some activity centres encourage more imaginative and cooperative play when they are close together. For example, if the block centre and

Well-defined, secluded play areas promote peer interaction.

dramatic play area are close together, children can use the blocks in their dramatic play.

- **Create a clear pathway through the room**
  To avoid children having to squeeze past tables or walk across established play areas, there should be a well-defined pathway that leads from one side of the room to the other. Knocking into other children or stepping on their toys won't encourage interaction!

Provide Space for the Three Kinds of Peer Groups

Type of Peer Group	Where/When they develop
Paired Interactions	• at tables for two • in private spaces • when games for two, like Checkers, are available
Casual Groups	• at sensory-creative tables (during activities such as playdough, fingerpaint, water and sand play) • in art areas • in floor play areas • at table toy areas (Solitary or parallel play is also seen in these areas)
Cooperative Groups	• in the dramatic play area • in the block area • in floor play areas

D. Getting Socially Isolated Children Involved in Peer Interactions

There are many things you can do to set the stage for peer interactions and to help children become part of a group.

Become Aware of How Much Teacher-Child Interaction There is

Children who have difficulty interacting with peers may spend a lot of time with you, perhaps too much. They may initiate interactions only with you because they are assured of getting a positive response. These children need to be encouraged to engage other children, and need to be reinforced when they do. A comment such as "Wow, you and Frankie are having a great time making that tower together!" lets a child know that he has your attention when he's engaged with peers, and not only when he is alone.

There is also a real danger of hovering over a child who is developmentally delayed and/or socially withdrawn, because he seems to need all the teacher input he can get. If there is a low teacher-child ratio in a classroom, children with special needs may spend too much time with their teachers. Research has shown that the more adults there are in a classroom, the less peer interaction there is!

Children who spend large amounts of time with you can benefit from situations in which you "Step In, Set Up and Fade Out!" (see the next section)

Step In, Set Up and Fade Out!

By setting up an interaction and then fading yourself out of the picture, you can help socially isolated children participate in peer interactions.

There are a number of ways to step in, set up and fade out:

- **Set up interactions from inside the group**
- **Set up interactions from outside the group**
- **Pair up two children**
- **Assign a collaborative task**
- **Direct conversations away from yourself**

Set up Interactions from Inside the Group

> *You are in the dramatic play area, and you are playing "Store" with three children. You see Anna, who usually plays alone, making tea for her dolls nearby. You decide to try to get her to join the group.*

**Remember:
If you want to get a child involved in pretend play, you have to play a pretend role yourself!**

> *"I see my friend Anna across the street!" you say to the children. "Hi Anna! We're so thirsty. Could we buy some drinks from you?" (It's important to continue playing a pretend role in this situation, to avoid being seen by the children as "the teacher" who is insisting that another child be admitted to their play.) Anna's face lights up, and she comes over, bringing some cups with her.*

> *"How much is the tea?" you ask. "Five dollars" she replies. "Okay! I'm so thirsty, I'll pay anything," you say. "Anybody here want a drink from Anna's store? She makes the best drinks in town!" The rest of the group follows your example, and Anna "sells" everyone a drink. You talk to her (in your pretend role) as if she really were a "drink seller," and when she seems to have become part of the group, you leave.*

> *"I have to catch my bus now," you say. "I'm going to visit my aunt. Thanks for all the lovely things, and thanks so much for the tea..." Then you fade out of the picture.*

The important thing to remember about helping a child join a peer group is — **don't ask the children "Can he/she play with you?"** It's too easy for them to say "No!" Rather create for the child a role which adds to the play and therefore makes his presence desirable.

Set up Interactions from Outside the Group

Sometimes you can help a child join a group without joining the group yourself.

> *During free play you notice Liam "bugging" the girls in the house centre. He keeps on driving his wagon into the wall of the "house", and they are getting very annoyed with him. You know that he's doing it for attention and that he lacks the social skills to initiate interactions in a positive manner.*

> *You approach him and make a suggestion quietly in his ear. He agrees and goes to get some toy tools, which he puts in his wagon. Then you both go back to the house centre and knock on the door. The girls say "Who's there?"*

> *Look at what happens . . .*

Help the child find a role that adds some fun to the play....

...fade away when you see they're doing okay!

Pair Up Two Children

Pairing a socially-withdrawn child with a sociable child can provide the less skilled child with some positive social experiences. This works best if you select a child who is the same age, is sociable, willing and has appropriate play skills.

The socially-skilled child instinctively makes adjustments to help the less social child take an active part in the interaction. He is likely to simplify his language, use more repetition and give instructions when necessary. In fact, he makes some of the same adjustments to his speech that caregivers make when interacting with young children.

> *Felix is a withdrawn 4-year-old with a language delay. Tim is a sociable, verbal 4-year-old. Because Felix is more interactive with Tim than with anyone else, every now and again his teachers pair the two boys up for activities. On one occasion, they asked the boys whether they wanted to go to the "secret hideaway" (a large appliance box) and explore the treasure box (a box full of interesting ornaments and trinkets). Felix and Tim examined and talked about the interesting objects they found in the box, and both really enjoyed themselves.*

The emphasis on pairing peers is not on the child with well-developed social skills helping or teaching the less skilled child. To prevent this, set the tone for a friendly interaction by using phrases like "play together," "find out together" or "cooperate" when introducing the children to the activity.

Assign a Collaborative Task

Much conversation and collaboration can result when a pair or small group of children complete an assigned task together. The best tasks are real-life ones, such as cleaning up a spill with a broom and dustpan, making a sign for the classroom, setting up a new toy or mixing the ingredients for a sensory activity. When you assign these tasks, each child should have a distinct role to play, and he shouldn't need help in order to complete it. In addition, the task should be set up so that a successful final product is possible only if each child contributes (which prevents the more competent children from doing it all themselves).

Collaborative tasks can bring about much positive interaction and a very good feeling among the children in the group, and the less social children feel more important and capable as a result. These tasks can accomplish a great deal, especially if they are assigned regularly so that the positive effects don't vanish as soon as the interaction is over.

There's a lot to talk about .....

....when you have a job to do together!

Direct Conversations Away from Yourself

In a group discussion, children may direct all their comments to you. You can easily become like an air-traffic controller, with all incoming and outgoing conversation being routed through you!

Use this situation to the children's advantage — redirect the conversation by drawing quieter children into the conversation and then fading yourself out. You can do this by asking questions, by making statements which a child can confirm and expand on, and by acting as interpreter for children who have difficulty making themselves understood.

By directing the conversation away from himself, the teacher is encouraging conversation among the children.

Encourage Outdoor Group Interactions

Outdoor activities which involve running, chasing, jumping and going down the slide enable children with good motor skills but limited social skills to interact successfully with their peers.

This kind of play is not very demanding for the less sociable child because it has few rules and involves little conversation. If the child is physically able to keep up, outdoor games can be extremely interactive.

Outdoor group-functional play provides opportunities for everyone to join in!

Set Up a Small Group — and Stay to Play

Many children can't go it alone, even when you step in, set up and fade out. They don't yet have the skills to stay involved in an interaction with other children, and as soon as you leave, they are no longer part of the group. These children need you to stay and support them during the interaction.

Start off small — perhaps just you and the child alone. A small corner with a few toys won't seem so overwhelming. Or you might join a small group of children who are already engaged in some activity. Make sure that the activity is appropriate to the child's level of play. If the child engages primarily in simple types of pretend play or in constructive play, start with that. Sociodramatic play may be cognitively too demanding for some children, particularly if they are language-delayed (see Chapter 9 for information on how to promote pretend play).

Once you and the child begin to interact, you can involve one or two children in your play or become involved in theirs.

You can keep the interaction going a number of ways:
- by following the children's lead and joining in their play
- by making suggestions that encourage interaction

  For example, "Let's drive our car over to Thomas's car and see what he's doing."
- by offering props that will create interaction

  For example, "Let's make a tunnel for all the cars to go under."
- by giving the child toys that will keep him involved

  For example, "Here's a man who wants a ride in your truck."

Children who rarely play with others may take a long time to warm up to their peers. At the beginning, there may be long periods of silence and little interaction. As long as these children are enjoying themselves and are being exposed to other children, they can still benefit from such interactions.

Raise the Profile of the Low-Profile Child

Children often form negative impressions of their less able peers, and these impressions can be hard to change. But unless they do change, the less social child remains at a serious disadvantage.

"She can't say anything," says Lara of Kelly, a language-delayed 4-year-old. "I don't wanna play with him," says Mohammed about Brian, a developmentally delayed 5-year-old. "He doesn't know how to play properly."

You can raise the profile of these less able children by helping their peers look at their disabilities in a different light.

> *Teacher: "You know, Lara, Kelly is still learning to talk and she's trying as hard as she can. Learning to talk is hard when you're just starting out. Some children learn to talk when they are small and others learn when they are bigger. It's like learning to ride a bike — my sister could ride a bike when she was 5, but I only learned when I was 7!"*

You can encourage children to find ways to interact with the less able child and to **want** to do it!

> *Teacher: "There are so many games you could play with Kelly that don't need talking, Lara. She loves running games and playing with 'goop.' I'll bet you could think of some activities that you could play with her, and you can let me know if you need anything for them."*

This gives Lara the opportunity to change her negative image of Kelly, because you have given **her** the responsibility for initiating positive interactions.

You can also give less social children high-profile jobs, like setting up an art table. In addition, show them a new toy first so that they feel like the "expert" when other children come to play with it.

Changing children's perceptions of their peers is a challenge. But if you can effect some change, you have gone along way to setting the stage for positive peer interactions.

Summary

There are many things teachers can do to help socially isolated children take part in peer interactions. They can create environments that have well-defined play areas and stimulating activities. They can set up interactive situations that make it easier for children to join in with their more sociable peers. They can also set up small groups where they themselves stay to play with the children, supporting those children whose social skills are limited. And they can make every effort to promote children's positive attitudes towards their less interactive and less verbal peers.

References

Adcock, D. & Segal, M. (1983). *Making friends.* Englewood Cliffs, NJ: Prentice-Hall.

Corsaro, W. A. (1981). Friendship in a nursery school: social organization in a peer environment. In S. R. Asher & J. M. Gottman (Eds.), *The development of children's friendships* (pp. 207-241) New York: Cambridge University Press.

Field, T. (1981). Early peer relations. In P. Strain (Ed.), *The utilization of classroom peers as behaviour change agents* (pp. 1-30). New York: Plenum.

Field, T., Roopnarine, J.L. & Segal, M. (Eds.), (1984). *Friendships in normal and handicapped children.* Norwood, NJ: Ablex.

Gallagher, T.M. (1991). Language and social skills: Implications for assessment and intervention with school-age children. In T, M. Gallagher, (Ed.), *Pragmatics of language: Clinical practice issues* (pp. 11-41). San Diego, CA: Singular.

Guralnick, M. (1982). Programmatic factors affecting child-child social interactions in mainstreamed preschool programs. In P.S. Strain (Ed.), *Social development of exceptional children* (pp. 71-91). Rockville, MD: Aspen.

Guralnick, M. (1986). The peer relations of young handicapped and nonhandicapped children. In P.S. Strain, M. Guralnick & H.M. Walker (Eds.), *Children's social behaviour: Development, assessment and modification* (pp. 93-140). New York: Academic Press.

Guralnick, M. (1990). Peer interactions and the development of handicapped children's social and communicative competence. In H. Foot, M.J. Morgan & R.H. Shute (Eds.) *Children helping children* (pp. 275-305). New York: John Wiley & Sons.

Hadley, P.A. & Rice, M. (1991). Conversational responsiveness of speech- and language-impaired preschoolers. *Journal of Speech and Hearing Research, 34,* (6), 1308-1317.

Hendrick, J. (1984). *The whole child.* St Louis: Times Mirror/Mosby.

Hildebrand, V. (1980). *Guiding young children.* New York: MacMillan.

Johnson, J.E., Christie, J.F. & Yawkey, T.D. (1987). *Play and early childhood development.* Glenview, IL: Scott, Foresman.

Kritchevsy, S., Prescott, E. & Walling, L. (1974). Planning environments for young children: Physical space. In G. Coates (Ed.), *Alternative learning environments* (pp. 311-320). Dowden: Hutchinson & Ross.

Levy, A.K. (1986). The language of play: The role of play in language development. In S. Burroughs and R. Evans (Eds.), *Play, language and socialization* (pp. 163-175). Cooper Station, NY: Gordon & Breach.

Loughlin, C.E. & Suina, J.H. (1982). *The learning environment: An instructional strategy.* New York: Teachers College Press.

Loughlin, C.E. & Martin, M.D. (1987). *Supporting literacy: developing effective learning environments.* New York: Teachers College Press.

Rice, M., Sell, M.A. & Hadley, P.A. (1991). Social interactions of speech- and language-impaired children. *Journal of Speech and Hearing Research, 34,* (6), 1299-1307.

Sachs, J., Goldman, J. & Chaille, C. (1985). Narratives in preschoolers sociodramatic play: The role of knowledge and communicative competence. In L. Galda and A.D. Pellegrini (Eds.), *Play, language and stories: The development of children's literate behaviour* (pp. 45-61). Norwood, NJ: Ablex.

Strain, P.S. (1982). Peer-mediated treatment of exceptional children's social withdrawal. In P.S. Strain (Ed.), *Social development of exceptional children* (pp. 93-105). Rockville, MD: Aspen.

P A R T   3

PROVIDE INFORMATION AND EXPERIENCE THAT PROMOTE LANGUAGE LEARNING

Social interaction with caring, responsive adults is crucial to children's development, but it needs more than social interaction for children to develop language. Part 3 of this book is about providing children with information and experiences that help them develop spoken language, not only to satisfy their physical and social needs but also to think, problem-solve, imagine and learn.

In Chapter 7, "Adjust the Way You Talk — And Help Children Develop Language", you will find clear, practical suggestions for helping children at each of the seven stages of language development. This chapter also addresses the needs of the second language learner.

Chapter 8, "Create an Environment for Talking and Learning", describes how children (from about 3 years onward) use language for planning, thinking, imagining and learning and shows how you can encourage such language use during your daily interactions and conversations.

Chapter 9, "Promote Pretend Play: Imagine the Fun, Imagine the Learning", contains information on the development of pretend play and its relationship to language. The chapter has many illustrated examples of what you can do to promote the development of pretend play and, in the process, foster language learning.

182

CHAPTER 7

Adjust the Way You Talk — And Help Children Develop Language

A. Children Learning Language: Cracking the Code and Figuring Out the Rules

By 14 months most children begin to express themselves using words. Although it may seem as if they are simply learning words, they aren't: what they are learning is a code.

Language is a code with a system of rules which children learn in a predictable sequence. (This sequence, which is reflected in the stages of language development, is described in Chapter 2.) Children learn which sounds are used, how these sounds are combined to form words and how words are combined into sentences according to the rules of grammar. There are a set number of rules to the code which, once learned by the child, can be applied to any number of sentences; this makes spoken language much more powerful and flexible than nonverbal communication.

The more rules of language a child has learned, the more adult-like his sentences sound.

No one ever sits down and teaches an infant that, for example, "my" goes before "bottle" or that "me" refers to herself. However, being an active learner, she identifies patterns in the language she hears and uses these to figure out t h e rules. She tests these rules by using them when speaking to others and, if they work, she uses them in other situations. For example, once she learns that the "my" in "my cookie" indicates that the cookie belongs to her, she uses it in sentences such as "my car", "my doggie", and "my Mama".

The rules of English grammar are quite tricky, and there are many exceptions to them. For example, we say "I pulled", I pushed", but not "I eated". However, children **do** say "I eated" because first they apply a general rule to every possible situation, and later they figure out the exceptions to each rule. By 5 years of age, children have changed and expanded their use of rules so that their sentences sound more and more adult-like.

Learning rules is an active process, spurred on by the child's search for meaning and her desire to communicate effectively. Your task is to make it easier for children to "crack the code" and learn language, especially for children who are language-delayed.

Researchers have found that, during interactions, caregivers use some general strategies which foster infants' language development. We can assume that these strategies, described below, have the potential to benefit all children at the early stages of language development.

> **1. Follow the Child's Lead**
>
> **2. Play Social Routines**
>
> **3. Use "Baby Talk"**

1. Follow the Child's Lead

When caregivers follow the infant's lead, they watch to see what her focus is and comment on it. That means that at the moment her attention is focused on something, she is receiving information about it.

The infant who is ready to "crack the code" can figure out the meaning of the words only if she can relate them to what she's focused on. Therefore, the caregiver's information must be clear and relevant. For example, if a 14-month-old baby were looking at another baby who was crying and the caregiver said "She's not too happy is she?", the infant would not be able to figure out how those words related to the baby's crying. But if the caregiver said "She's **crying**! Samantha's **crying**!", the infant would find it much easier to make the connection between the label and the baby's action.

2. Play Social Routines

Because social routines are so repetitive and predictable, the infant has many opportunities to figure out the meaning of the caregiver's words. Eventually she imitates these words and, in time, uses them spontaneously, first during the routine and then in other situations. Many infants "crack the code" and use their first words as a result of their participation in social routines.

3. Use "Baby Talk"

"Baby Talk" has a bad reputation. Many people say that you should talk to babies like you talk to anyone else. If you aren't sure about this, try the following experiment:

Talk to a preschooler, and immediately afterwards talk to a baby **exactly the same way.**

Can you do it?

Not unless you make a conscious effort — and even then, it probably feels very strange.

That's because adults instinctively talk to infants in **Motherese,** which is a special way mothers have been found to talk to their babies.

When using Motherese, caregivers:

- vary their tone of voice, using a higher than normal pitch

- emphasize key words

- shorten sentences

- simplify their messages, using simpler grammar as well as vocabulary such as "doggie" for "dog"

- use a slower rate of speech, with longer pauses between words

- use a great deal of repetition

Let's put your **hat on**, Michael, ok? Put your **hat on**?

When you use "Baby Talk", it's natural to say the same thing over and over again.

Motherese or "Baby Talk" has a serious purpose, and that is to connect and communicate with infants. Motherese makes it easier for caregivers to gain and hold the child's attention and express their positive emotions toward her.

Caregivers use less and less "Baby Talk" as children's language develops.

Boom Boom Boom!

Boom! Boom! You're banging the drum!

Wow, you're a really good drummer! You could be in a band!

"Baby Talk" also makes language easier to understand. Like a tourist in a foreign country, a baby finds it easier to learn language when people speak slowly, emphasize key words, simplify and repeat their messages. Once the child learns to talk and develops more advanced language skills, "Baby Talk" becomes unnecessary and fades out of the picture.

In the next sections, we take a look at the specific adjustments you can make in the way you talk to children at different stages of development.

B. Adjust Your Language for Children at Stages 1 and 2

Children at Stages 1 and 2 (birth — 8 months) haven't yet developed intentional communication and they can't understand what you say. But they do listen to the "music" in your voice and the intonation patterns you use. You will find yourself using "Baby Talk" with children at these stages of development (see Chapter 4 for information on "Reduce Conversational Overload").

• **Comment on what the child seems to be telling you**
Because infants at Stages 1 and 2 aren't attending to the meaning of specific words, your sentences can be longer and less repetitive than they will be once children start to understand words.

Cheryl speaks in fairly long sentences to Sammy, varying her tone of voice and speaking a little slower than usual to keep his attention.

C. Adjust Your Language for Children at Stage 3

Children at Stage 3 (8 — 13 months) are moving toward cracking the code and using their first words. You can help them do this by supplying the words for their nonverbal messages (interpreting) and providing them with simple information about things of interest to them. At this stage it is important for your sentences to become shorter and more repetitive than they were with children at Stages 1 and 2.

For Children at Stage 3

> Once the child shows an interest in objects and events and becomes aware of the meaning of some words in specific situations, adjust your language and:
>
> • INTERPRET what the child is telling you
>
> • LABEL the things in which the child shows interest
>
> • MATCH YOUR COMMENTS to the child's focus
>
> • COMMENT on the child's actions and use GESTURES
>
> • COMMENT on the child's actions and use "FUN WORDS"
>
> • Use the PROPER NAMES of objects — instead of "it", "that", "this" or "them"

• **INTERPRET what the child is telling you**

Sometimes INTERPRETING the child's message takes the form of a question, but the child still hears the words he needs to learn.

• **LABEL the things in which the child shows interest**

When Ben is interested in something, Tina LABELS the object for him, using as few words as possible. This helps him develop both receptive language (the word is new for him) and expressive language (he'll try to say it eventually).

• **MATCH YOUR COMMENTS** to the child's focus

Michael is excited that he finally got the puzzle piece in, but Eileen's comment doesn't match his focus.

Now Eileen has MATCHED HER COMMENT to Michael's focus.

For Children at Stage 3

• **COMMENT on the child's actions and use GESTURES**

By using GESTURES and the word at the same time, Paula helps Faisel figure out what she means.

Pull! Pull the string!

Gestures are fun, and they make it easier for children to understand you. At Stages 3 and 4, it's easier for children to use gestures than to use words which is why young children wave "bye-bye" and pretend to blow when something is "hot" long before they say the words. Of course, as soon as the child shows you she understands the word, the gesture becomes unnecessary.

So act it out — and let the children see what you're saying.

Remember to:

• be face-to-face with the child
• be consistent in the gestures you use
• use the word at the same time as the gesture
• repeat yourself

• **COMMENT on the child's actions and use "FUN WORDS"**

Claire uses "FUN WORDS" when commenting on Andrew's actions; she knows they are fun for him to listen to, are easy to understand and are often easier than real words to imitate.

Squish! Squish!

For Children at Stage 3

• Use the PROPER NAMES of objects — instead of "it", "that", "this" or "them."

Christa knows what a ball is and how to use it, but she doesn't know how to say "ball"; so her teacher should use the PROPER NAME and say "Come on! Give me _the ball_!"

The teacher should say "Good girl, you rolled _the ball_!"

The teacher should say "Get ready! Here comes _the ball_!"

D. Adjust Your Language for Children at Stage 4

Children at Stage 4 (12 — 18 months) can:

- use a number of single words (these are **expressive language** skills)

- understand a number of words (these are **receptive language** skills)

For Children at Stage 4

In order to help children at Stage 4 develop both their expressive and receptive language skills:

- **LABEL** the things in which the child shows interest

- **CONFIRM** the child's message by **IMITATING** or **PROVIDING A CORRECT MODEL**

- **EXPAND** on what the child has said by repeating her message and adding a few words

- **EXTEND** the topic by providing information that increases the child's understanding

When you respond to children at Stage 4, you often use more than one technique at a time:

Step 1 — Confirm the child's message by imitating or providing a correct model

Step 2 — Expand by repeating her message and adding a few words

First Cindy CONFIRMS Tony's message by providing a correct model and then EXPANDS by adding a few words to what he said.

When you provide the child with a **language model**, you say what she said, but you say it correctly. In this way, you maintain the flow of conversation and, at the same time, provide information that helps her learn the correct rule.

When you **expand** on what the child says, you show her how to add more information to her message. **You repeat what she said, but add one or two words of your own** to form a more complete phrase or sentence. This helps her learn rules for constructing more complete and complex sentences.

When you respond to children at Stage 4, you may combine two other techniques:

Step 1 — Expand on what the child said by repeating her message and adding a few words; and then

Step 2 — Extend the topic by providing information that increases the child's understanding (This is discussed in more detail in Chapter 8.)

Karin first EXPANDS on Juan's message. She then EXTENDS the topic by telling him what she's going to do.

E. Adjust Your Language for Children at Stages 5, 6 and 7

The techniques used with children at Stage 4 apply to children at Stages 5, 6 and 7 too. When you label, model, expand and extend the topic, you are promoting their expressive and receptive language development. (The kind of "teacher talk" that helps children develop more advanced and complex language skills is described in Chapter 8.)

Even when children can speak in sentences, they still need to hear correct models, expansions and extensions.

F. Tell the Children What's Happening in the World

There are many things that you can tell children which give them important information about their world. They may not understand it all at first, but with time and repetition, it will make sense.

Label Objects, People, Actions and Events

Your labels and descriptions of everyday events are important for young language learners. If you provide an infant with the label "Bib" every time you put on her bib, it won't take her too long to connect the word with the object. When you talk about what you or others are doing, such as "I'm washing my hands" or "I'm cleaning the table", children gain important information.

All this information helps children build up a store of receptive language which they will eventually use themselves.

Don't move in without warning — tell the child what's going to happen.

Provide Explanations, Especially When Things Go Wrong!

When things go wrong, teachers may not think to give the children an explanation, as in the example below when the children's pizza disappears.

These teachers discussed with each other what was wrong with the pizza, but they didn't discuss it with the children.

These are still too hot.

I thought I had let them cool long enough...

They should cool for at least 10 minutes...

A simple explanation clears up the confusion.

Too hot! Too hot! Pizzas are too hot!

Let them have their drinks while these cool down.

Have your drinks first and then the pizzas will be cool.

If we are to encourage children's curiosity and questions, it's important to provide them with simple explanations for things in which they are interested but don't understand.

Jame's crying because he fell and hurt himself.

Sean wants to know why James is crying, and so Valerie gives him a simple explanation.

G. Make It Easier for Language-delayed Children to Learn Language

Children who have a language delay find it difficult to learn the rules of language, especially grammatical rules. A 3- or 4-year-old with a language delay may speak in sentences of only a few words, and at more advanced stages of language development, her sentences may contain grammatical errors which her peers have already outgrown.

Correcting these children's errors won't help at all. For example, a language-delayed child may say "Him's sitting in my chair." You may tell her "Kelly, it's not 'Him's sitting in my chair'; it's '**He's** sitting in my chair'", but she will probably make the same error one minute later. This is because she has not yet learned the correct grammatical rule for use of pronouns.

In addition to grammatical errors, you may have noticed that children with language delays confuse word meanings. For example, a child may say "Stand down" when she means "Sit down".

Think, for a moment, how confusing it must be for these children to figure out the rules of language when they receive so much information at one time. Obviously, the adjustments we make for normally-developing children aren't enough to help children who have language delays. Therefore, we must make further adjustments to the way we talk to these children.

By using the following techniques, you can help children with language delays learn both vocabulary and grammatical rules during everyday conversations.

- **Provide intensive repetition**
  Make it easier for the child to figure out a grammatical rule by repeating sentences illustrating the rule again and again within a short space of time.

> **Child:** *Him don't got no mitts (pointing to a child who is not wearing mitts).*
>
> **Teacher:** ***He** has no mitts? I wonder why. **He** has mitts (points to another child), and **he** has mitts (points to another child), and **he** has mitts (points to another child), but Bradley has no mitts. Maybe **he** left them at home.*

This teacher provided the child with five examples of "he" in less than a minute. If this kind of repetition is provided throughout the day in natural conversations, the child has a better chance of learning the rule. However, don't provide intensive repetition for every rule the child has difficulty with. Choose one or two and stick with those.

> *Remember: It is easier for a child to learn an earlier-developing grammatical rule (described in Chapter 2 in the sections on Expressive Language at Stages 5 or 6) than a later-developing one (described in Chapter 2 in the section on Expressive Language at Stage 7).*

- **The timing of your response should correspond with the child's focus of attention**
  Timing is critical! At the early stages of language development, children learn best when the information they hear relates exactly to what they are experiencing at that moment in time.

For example, when a cup falls off the table, a child may say, "Fall down." If the teacher immediately says "The cup fell down. I see that! The cup fell down," her input is well-timed.

If, however, the teacher picks up the cup, puts it back on the table, wipes up the spill and then says "The cup fell down. On the floor! The cup fell down," she has missed the boat. The child's focus has moved on to something else, making it less likely that she will learn from the model provided.

- **Slow down**
  A language-delayed child will find it easier to process and learn language when you talk at a slower rate than normal. A slower rate of speech will enable her to pay closer attention to the way your sentence is phrased and help her to figure out the rule.

- **Position the word or words that the child needs to hear at the beginning or end of the sentence (not in the middle) and exaggerate them**
  If, for example, you are stressing the rule "verb-ing" (e.g., "I am **eating**") to indicate ongoing action, consider how clearly the "ing" can be heard and processed by the child in the following two examples:

  Example 1

  > *Teacher:* Look, Adam is **playing** *(pause),*
  > *and Jessica is* **playing** *(pause),*
  > *and Samara is* **playing** *(pause),*
  > *and Nathan is* **watching.**

  Example 2

  > *Teacher:* Look, Adam is playing in the playground, and Jessica is playing with him, and Samara is playing with him, and Nathan is watching them.

  It's easier for children to pay attention to words at the beginning or end of a sentence. In the middle of the sentence, the words may get lost.

- **Use contrasts to highlight the rule**
  Children often confuse words or phrases that have something in common. For example, they may say "stand down" for "sit down".

  It helps the child to figure out the rule if you contrast the two phrases.

  > *Teacher:* Look Tammy, we're all going to **sit down.** *Jonathon, you* **sit down** *(pause while Jonathon sits down), and Dan, you* **sit down** *(pause while Dan sits down), and Bella, you* **sit down** *(pause while Bella sits down). But I'm not going to sit down — I'm going to* **stand up.** *(Teacher stands up while the others are sitting down.)*

  This kind of contrast makes the rule a lot clearer to the child. This technique also helps children figure out grammatical rules which are confusing, such as use of the pronoun "he" for males and "she" for females.

- **Use real-life situations in which the child has a real interest**
  Because children use grammatical rules to send real messages, they must learn them in purposeful, real-life situations.

H. Second Language Learning: A Complex Process

All children have a first language, which is any language learned before age 3. A language learned after age 3 is considered to be a second language.

When a child younger than 3 years of age learns two (sometimes more) languages at the same time, this is referred to as **simultaneous bilingualism.**

A child who learns a second language after age 3 goes through **sequential bilingualism,** which involves a different process of learning from simultaneous bilingualism.

Simultaneous bilingualism

When infants are exposed to two languages in infancy, there are two patterns of exposure: they either experience a "one-person, one-language" situation where the mother speaks one language and the father another, or they experience a situation where both parents speak both languages. The "one-person, one-language" has been found to help children separate and learn the two languages.

Three stages of language learning can be identified in children who learn two first languages in infancy:

Stage 1

Infants who are exposed to two languages "mix" the two into one system — e.g., an infant learning Spanish and English may call a "kitty cat" a "kitty-gato" or may use words from both languages in a short sentence.

Stage 2

Around 2½ years of age, the child starts to separate the words belonging to each language and recognizes to which person each language should be spoken.

While learning the two languages, the child often uses whole phrases or sentences which she imitates and memorizes, such as "I wanna" and "Gimme dat." In addition, she engages in "copy-catting", which involves imitation of another person's speech and actions. Both these strategies help her interact with others and eventually learn the rules of the language.

Stage 3

When one language is used more than the other (as is often the case), that language becomes dominant. By 7 years of age, the child can cope with the two language systems without difficulty, using both vocabulary and grammar appropriately for her age.

Sequential Bilingualism

When a child learns a second language after age 3, she has already figured out the basic rules of her first language, and this helps her learn the second language. She knows how to have conversations and is cognitively more mature than the infant learning two languages simultaneously. This child's task is to add a second language to the one she already has, a task which takes years to accomplish. When a child over the age of 3 enters an environment where a second language is spoken, it takes approximately 3 months for her to begin to understand the second language, about 2 years to be able to carry on a conversation and 5 to 7 years to be able to think in the second language.

There are three stages of second language learning which seem to motivate and guide these learners:

Stage 1:

The child becomes involved in social interactions with speakers of the second language.

During this stage, the child relies on whole, memorized phrases and sentences — e.g., "Know what?" or "All right, you guys." She also uses nonverbal communication — e.g., pointing, and a number of key words which are useful in social situations. In general, she tries to act as if she knows what's going on and guesses a lot at what people mean.

Stage 2:

The child communicates with second language speakers in the second language.

The principle at this stage seems to be "Start talking." The child begins to create her own sentences, which may include memorized phrases and some new vocabulary. She communicates as best she can, even if the way she expresses herself is not correct. Children who are risk-takers learn the language quicker than those who don't talk much for fear of making a mistake.

Stage 3:

The child attempts to speak correctly, using correct vocabulary, grammar and pronunciation.

The child looks for patterns in sentences, just as she did when learning her first language, and then works out the rules.

"Should I Be Concerned?": Normal Patterns of Language Use in Second Language Learners

Many children who are second language learners are thought to be language-delayed when, in fact, they are demonstrating normal second language characteristics.

The following characteristics are commonly seen in second language learners:

- **a silent period**
  Children who speak one language and are learning a second language may say very little for up to seven months! It seems that they need this "silent period" to build up their knowledge of the new language before they try to use it.

- **code mixing**
  Children often use words from both languages in one sentence.

- **loss of the first language**
  If the child has learned a first language but doesn't use it much, she will lose her skills in that language. This means that while English is still being learned, her ability in both languages will be below age level.

- **lots of grammatical errors**
  When a child learns a second language sequentially, expect to hear many grammatical errors until she figures out all the rules of the language.

I. Support Second Language Learners

Children who come to child care speaking little or no English must experience feelings of isolation, confusion and frustration. Fortunately, as their teacher, you are able to support their efforts to learn a second language and to become what we would all like to become — fully bilingual.

There are a number of ways to support a second language learner. You can support their first language, make them feel comfortable in their strange new surroundings and talk to them in ways that help them figure out the rules of English.

Promote the Use of the Child's First Language at Home and at Child Care

It was once thought that the best way to help children learn their second language was to expose them only to that language. But the experts tell us that this was incorrect: the better developed the child's first language, the easier it is for her to learn a second language. In light of what we now know, it has become clear that the best way to foster second language learning is to support the child's **first** language.

- **Children under the age of 5, who are learning one language at home and another at child care should be exposed to their first language as much as possible**

When parents aren't sure which language to speak to their child, we can safely encourage them to speak their first language. This is quite a relief because if parents are advised to speak to their children in a language which they don't speak fluently, interactions will suffer; parents may interact less with their children and will probably have less to say when they do.

By speaking to their child in her first language, parents are laying a solid foundation for the second. Without this support, both first and second language learning could be delayed and disrupted. By 5 years of age, the child has a fairly well-established first language. While she can certainly benefit from exposure to her first language, she will not be at-risk for language problems in the same way that a younger child with a poorly-developed first language will be.

- **If more than one language is used in the home with a child under age 3, "one person, one language" is best**

If children hear both caregivers speak two languages, they become confused. "One person, one language" reduces such confusion.

- **Promote the child's first language at child care**

If you and the child are fortunate enough to speak the same first language, speak it to her! And if there are other children in the room with the same first language, encourage them to talk together. Consider enlisting the help of volunteers who will play and interact with the child in her first language.

Te has gól piato?
Tu estaras bien.

It's wonderful when the teacher can comfort a child in that child's first language.

Make Second Language Learners Feel Special

Children who come to child care speaking another language and not speaking any English need to feel accepted and liked, and they need to like **you**! This will have an enormous impact on how successfully they learn their new language.

The following three factors are critical to successful second language learning :

- **motivation to learn**
- **feelings of self-confidence**
- **low level of anxiety**

Let's picture Tanya, 3 years old, who is newly-arrived from Russia. She speaks no English, and is in the preschool room with fifteen other preschoolers none of whom speak Russian.

Tanya keeps to herself and seldom initiates interactions with teachers or peers. One of her teachers, Novea, makes a point of establishing a close relationship with her, giving her a great deal of support and affection and spending some time playing with her every day. When Tanya attempts to communicate with Novea in Russian, Novea responds as best she can and never demands that Tanya try to say anything in English. Novea also encourages peer interaction by inviting other children to join their play and then fading herself out.

As a result of all this positive interaction, Tanya has:

- a great deal of motivation to communicate with her teachers and peers
- the self-confidence to seek out others in her new environment
- a low level of anxiety

Within 6 months, Tanya is using some common single words. She has also learned some phrases like "Know what?" and "You wanna play?" She is on her way to mastering her second language.

Make Your Input Easy To Understand

The most important thing about talking to a child who is learning English as a second language is:

Make your language easy to understand

Children will learn only if they can make sense of what they hear. This explains why watching TV programs in a second language or overhearing conversations between two second language speakers doesn't help people learn the language. If you can't understand it, you can't learn from it. It's that simple!

Your task is to make it possible for the child to understand you. Once you have that goal in mind, you automatically make all sorts of adjustments and adaptations (as described in the first part of this chapter). And come to think about it, the way you talk will sound an awful lot like the way you talk to children learning their first language! You make yourself interesting to listen to and provide information that the child can understand and learn from.

Even though Kinue doesn't understand English, she has a good idea of what her teacher is saying.

Kinue's teacher helps her understand what he is saying because he:

- uses grammatically simple sentences
- uses simple, everyday vocabulary
- repeats what he has said
- talks about what's happening in the here-and-now
- exaggerates important words
- uses gestures
- slows down

Use Music to Help the Child Learn a Second Language

Because second language learners imitate whole phrases and sentences and use them to communicate, music can help them learn new phrases and sentences.

For example:

> Tommy Thumb, Tommy Thumb
> Where are you?
> Here I am, here I am
> And how do you do?

The sentences **"Where are you?"** and **"Here I am"** can be modelled for the child in interactive situations so she understands what they mean and can use them herself when appropriate.

Not only is music a wonderful way of making contact with children but it also helps them learn language.

Summary

The quality and quantity of language that children are exposed to during their everyday interactions with their caregivers has a significant impact on their language development. When learning both first and second languages, children have to make sense of what they hear and figure out the rules of the language. Caregivers help children do this when they adjust the way they talk, making language easy to understand at the early stages of language development and adding more information as the child's ability progresses. Teachers can make this process easier for children with language delays by providing intensive repetition, slowing down their rate of speech and highlighting the important words. Second language learners are supported by teachers who make them feel comfortable in their new surroundings and promote their first language both at home and, when possible, at the child care centre.

References

Barnes, S., Gutfreund, M., Satterly, D. & Wells, G. (1983). Characteristics of adult speech which predict children's language development. *Journal of Child Language, 10,* 65-84.

Bloom, L & Lahey, M. (1978). *Language development and language disorders.* New York: John Wiley & Sons.

Bozinou-Doukas, E. (1983). Learning disability: The case of the bilingual child. In D.R. Omark & J. G. Erickson (Eds.), *The bilingual exceptional child* (pp. 213-232). San Diego: College Hill Press.

Chud, G. & Fahlman, R. (1985). *Early childhood education for a multicultural society.* University of British Columbia: Western Education Development Group.

Craig, H. K. (1983). Applications of pragmatic language models for intervention. In T. M. Gallagher & C. A. Prutting (Eds.), *Pragmatic Assessment and Intervention Issues in Language* (pp. 101 - 127). San Diego: College Hill Press.

Cross, T.G. (1978). Mothers' speech and its association with rate of linguistic development in young children. In N. Waterson & C. Snow (Eds.), *The development of communication* (pp. 199-216). New York: John Wiley & Sons.

Cummins, J. (1981). *Bilingualism and minority-language children.* Toronto: OISE Press.

Dumtschin, J.U. (1988). Recognize language development and delay in early childhood. *Young Children, March,* 16-24.

Esling, J.H. (Ed.), (1989). *Multicultural education and policy: ESL in the 1990s.* Toronto: OISE Press.

Farran, D.C. (1982). Mother-child interaction, language development and the school performance of poverty children. In L. Feagans and D.C. Farran (Eds.), *The language of children reared in poverty* (pp. 19-48). New York: Academic Press.

Ferguson, C.A. (1977). Baby talk as a simplified register. In C.E. Snow & C.A. Ferguson (Eds.), *Talking to children: Language input and acquisition* (pp. 219-235). London: Cambridge University Press.

Houston, M.W. (1990). Teaching English as a second language through daily programming. In Kenise Murphy Kilbride (Ed.). *Multicultural early childhood education: A discovery approach for teachers* (pp. 64-68), School of Early Childhood Education, Ryerson Polytechnic Institute, Toronto.

Kessler, C. (1984). Language acquisition in bilingual children. In N. Miller, (Ed.) *Bilingualism and language disability: Assessment and remediation* (pp. 26-54). San Diego: College Hill Press.

Krashen, S. (1982). *Principles and practice in second language acquisition.* New York: Pergamon Press.

Lasky, E.Z. & Klopp, K. (1982). Parent-child interactions in normal and language-disordered children. *Journal of Speech and Hearing Disorders, 47*(1), 7-18.

McLaughlin, B. (1984). *Second-language acquisition in childhood: Volume 1. Preschool children.* Hillsdale, N.J.: Lawrence Erlbaum Associates.

Newport, E., Gleitman, H & Gleitman, L. (1977). Mother, I'd rather do it myself: Some effects and non-effects of maternal speech style. In C. E. Snow & C.A. Ferguson (Eds.), *Talking to children* (pp. 109-149). London: Cambridge University Press.

Owens, R.E. (1984). *Language development: An introduction.* Columbus, Ohio: Charles E. Merrill.

Roseberry-McKibbin, C, Eicholtz, G. & McCaffrey, P (1990). *Second language acquisition: Differentiating language differences from language disorders.* Miniseminar at American Speech-Hearing Association Annual Convention, Seattle, Washington.

Snow, C.E. (1984). Parent-child interaction and the development communicative ability. In R.L. Schiefelbusch & J. Pickar (Eds.), *The acquisition of communicative competence* (pp. 69-107). Baltimore: University Park Press.

Snow, C., Midkiff-Borunda, S., Small, A., & Proctor, A. (1984). Therapy as social interaction: Analyzing the contexts for language remediation. *Topics in Language Disorders, 4*(4), 72-85.

Weismer, S.E. (1991). Theory and Practice: A principled approach to treatment of young children with specific language disorders. *National Student Speech Language Hearing Association Journal,* 18, 76-86.

Wells, J.L. (1980). *Children's language and learning.* Englewood Cliffs, NJ: Prentice Hall.

C H A P T E R   8

Create an Environment for Talking and Learning

A. Learning to Talk: A Social Act

Learning to talk involves becoming a social being. It's a way of making oneself heard, of becoming part of a group, part of a community and part of a culture.

When a child begins to talk, he talks mainly to satisfy his social needs. Language is used to get and keep an interaction going and to talk about things in the here-and-now.

As the caregiver confirms, models, expands and extends the topic of the conversation during these early conversations, she becomes, in the child's eyes, more than a social partner; she becomes a resource, someone from whom the child can get information.

As the child becomes a better conversation partner, there is a change in the quantity and quality of his conversations with his caregivers. Conversations occur more often and last longer. More information is exchanged, and the child asks more questions. He doesn't talk only about the here-and-now; he talks about what happened yesterday, what will happen tomorrow and what might happen if....

The child is no longer simply learning to talk.

He is talking to learn.

Children start out using language to satisfy their social needs; in time language becomes a tool for thinking, problem-solving and learning.

B. Talking to Learn: Using Language to Think and Learn About the World

Listen to preschoolers and kindergartners having a conversation and you'll hear them talk about much more than the here-and-now.

They use language to:

- **Go beyond the here-and-now**
  They talk about the past and the future.

- **Go beyond their own personal experience**
  They use language to project themselves into situations, and they consider how they or others would feel or react to these situations (for example, what it would be like to go to the moon or to be as strong as..., as big as..., as famous as..., as tall as...); they also think about possible explanations for things that they don't quite understand.

- **Go beyond the real world into the imagined world**
  With language, children can bring their imagined ideas to life.

The preschoolers at Greenfield Child Care Centre are playing outdoors. The ground is muddy after a night of rain. Matty, who has been digging in the mud for the last few minutes, suddenly sees an earthworm wriggling under the surface. He gets very excited and picks it up with a stick, yelling to the other children "Look, I got a worm!" Five other boys run over to see the worm, and soon they are all digging for earthworms.

What children have to say about worms tells us a lot about how they think and try to understand the world.

Let's listen in to Matty and Liam's conversation.

Matty: *Don't dig so hard. You'll break the worms in half if you do that!* (beyond the here-and-now)

Liam: *Break them in half! Ha! You can't break a worm in half.*

Matty: *You can. But if you break an earthworm in half, he won't die. He'll grow a new head and a new body and there will be two worms.* (beyond personal experience)

Liam: *Who said?*

Matty: *My mom read me a book about worms.* (beyond the here-and-now)

Liam: *Here's one! I got one!*

Matty: *Look how long yours is! He's longer than mine. He must eat a lot or maybe he's just older.* (beyond personal experience)

Liam: *Yeah, maybe he's older.*

Matty: *It's so dark down there. How does he find his food? He probably uses a flashlight! (Laughs)* (beyond the real world)

Liam: *Yeah, a big flashlight! (Laughs)*

Not all preschool children have Matty's ability to use language. Liam can barely keep up with him. Matty is the kind of child who's always asking questions, thinking about what he sees and hears, wondering how things work and reflecting on his experiences — and he uses language to do this. He has developed not only excellent language skills, but also a way of using language to analyze and understand the world.

Children can't learn to use language like this without lots of help. Matty has learned it from those important adults in his life, who model and promote the use of language to problem-solve, plan, predict, reason and imagine. In so doing they have helped him develop "the language of learning", which he has internalized and now uses quite naturally.

Because the ability to analyze and reflect upon the world is so critical to successful learning, all children need to develop "the language of learning." When they begin to talk about things that are beyond the

> **The way children use language is learned from the important adults in their lives. When children hear adults use language to think, problem-solve, plan, predict, reason and imagine during their conversations, they learn to use language for the same purposes.**

here-and-now (usually around age 2), they are ready to start talking to learn.

The most important things you can help children learn are: to think and analyze, to problem-solve, to plan, to predict, to reason and to imagine. These uses for language should be integrated into both your everyday interactions with the children and into your programming. Although many children with language delays have difficulty understanding language that goes beyond the here-and-now, they too need some exposure to this kind of talk if they are to learn to use it themselves.

C. Encouraging the "Language of Learning" during Conversations

There are many different aspects of language use that children can learn during their conversations with you.

Clarify Word Meanings during Conversations

Sometimes children don't know what they're talking about!

David is 5 years old and is in the kindergarten class at Sunnyview Child Care Centre. Once a week they use the equipment in the gym, and whenever they do, their teacher always says "Everybody remember to use common sense when you're in the gym!" David came home and told his mother what his teacher had said. "What's common sense?" his mother asked. "I don't know," he replied, "but we're supposed to use it every time we go to the gym." What confusion!

David's mother tried to explain to him what common sense meant, but she knew that even after her explanation, he was still confused. So she made a point of using the word during conversations. When David's older sister wanted to wear her spring jacket when the temperature was minus five, his mother commented: "Your sister is really not using her common sense. That jacket isn't nearly warm enough for such cold weather. She's going to freeze!"

The next day, David said, "I'm using common sense today. I'm wearing my warm jacket to daycare 'cos it's so cold outside." "Yes, you are using common sense," said his mother. "That way, you know you'll stay warm. And I'm going to use common sense too. I'm going to fill up the car with gas on the way to daycare so we don't run out of gas in this freezing cold weather."

And so, after many, many conversations and discussions about common sense, David's understanding of "common sense" increased. But he won't understand it fully until he is in his teens.

Many words and expressions are confusing to children hearing them for the first time.

Young children often use words that they don't really understand. A child may say that something is "disgusting," or that he's got "the 'flu" or ask "why?" without understanding the meanings of the words.

There are many words whose meanings are difficult to explain. But by having conversations with children and by providing them with the information they need, you can help them change or expand their understanding of word meanings. That's the beauty of conversations — there's so much learning going on without much teaching.

Use Children's Questions to Help Them Make Connections

When children ask questions, they create the ideal conditions for learning: they draw you into conversations and obtain valuable information from your responses. And the questions they ask give you a bird's-eye view into the workings of their minds, as in the example illustrated below:

Kevin's question makes it obvious that his concept of "feet" doesn't include the concept of "feet" that is used in measurement.

Don't worry, Kevin. It's only 3 feet deep.

Three big feet or three little feet?

Kevin's teacher can help him understand the other meaning for "foot" by:

- providing a simple on-the-spot explanation for the meaning of a "foot" as it relates to measurement

- giving him rulers and tape measures to examine so he becomes familiar with the length of a "foot"

- measuring things or people

- using the word "foot" meaningfully in future conversations

If children seldom ask questions, they miss critical opportunities to talk things through with another person and so gain a better understanding of the world.

We have to wonder whether children who don't ask questions are reluctant to interact or haven't learned to use language to reflect on the world with interest and curiosity. Either way, the child's intellectual development is likely to suffer. Those are the children who need your help to discover the wonders of the world.

> *If children seldom ask questions, they miss critical opportunities to talk things through with another person and so gain a better understanding of the world.*

Wonder About The World Together

Most young children think that adults know everything, but sooner or later they'll find out the truth — and there is good reason to disillusion them early on. We want children to think that learning is a wonderful, never-ending process and that adults *don't* know everything! We want them to realize that adults also wonder about how things work, what things mean and why they happen. The best way to encourage this attitude is to model being an active, curious learner yourself.

You can encourage an attitude of learning and discovering by:

- **admitting to not knowing things** when children ask you questions and suggesting that you find out the answer together

- **searching for answers to questions with the child** through experiments, looking in books or asking someone who knows

- **wondering aloud about things that interest or puzzle you** and getting excited about the small wonders of the world, like a spider's web or a bird in a tree

- **stressing the many possible solutions and answers to questions** and downplaying "right" and "wrong" answers

When you and the children question and search for answers together, discuss ideas, consider possibilities and share the small wonders of the world, then you have created an environment for talking and learning.

This approach can be hard for teachers because it means not correcting children's mistakes right away, not asking too many "fact" questions (see Chapter 4, page 130) and not giving all the answers.

But just because you're not teaching doesn't mean that the children aren't learning. They are. Look at some of the ideas Barbara and Phillip came up with together...

Extending the Topic and Enriching the Child's Understanding

In Chapter 7, the idea of extending the topic was introduced. With children at more advanced stages of language development, extending the topic is an important strategy which plays a major role in talking to learn.

When you extend the topic, you provide additional information which increases the child's understanding. This often involves going beyond the here-and-now, and beyond concepts such as colours, shapes, sizes and textures.

When you respond to children's initiations and use language to talk about past and future, to think about reasons and explanations, to project into others' experiences and to imagine and pretend, you are extending the topic.

There's a lot more to a rabbit
Than his colour, shape and size.
You could talk about his twitchy nose
And about his big, sad eyes.
You could imagine how it feels
To be stuck inside a cage,
And what it's like to have no mother
At such an early age.
You could compare him to a hamster,
To a dog, a mouse, a cat.
You could talk about the importance
Of a very gentle pat.
You could wonder what would happen
If he ever ran away.
There's so much to interest children,
So much they'd have to say!

Extending the Topic

When you are having a conversation with a child, you have a number of options for extending the topic:

INFORM • give information about past or present • provide details • compare/contrast two things • relate present experience to past experience	**PROJECT** • project into other people's lives, experiences • project into situations never experienced (What might it be like to....?)
EXPLAIN • give reasons • explain outcomes • describe cause-effect relationships • draw conclusions • justify actions, opinions • recognize problem and provide solutions	**TALK ABOUT THE FUTURE** • talk about what will happen • talk about what might happen • predict what will happen • anticipate possible problems and possible solutions • consider alternative ways of handling a situation
TALK ABOUT FEELINGS • talk about how one feels • talk about opinions, impressions	**PRETEND/IMAGINE** • talk about imaginary things • play a pretend role • create an imaginary "story" (based on real life or fantasy)

Take the child's stage of language development into consideration when you extend the topic: the information you provide to children at Stage 5 will be less complex than the information you provide to those at Stages 6 and 7.

Respond to the child's "Sssshhh! She's sleeping" and extend the topic by:

INFORMING

"Your baby is sleeping in her bed just like you sleep on your cot." (comparing)

PROJECTING

"If I were that baby, I'd like you to sing me a song while I went to sleep."

EXPLAINING

"I'll be quiet so I don't wake the baby."

Sssshhh! She's sleeping.

TALKING ABOUT FEELINGS

"You'll be mad at me if I wake your baby."

PRETENDING

"I'm tired too. I'm going to sleep right next to the baby." (Lies down and pretends to sleep).

TALKING ABOUT THE FUTURE

"When that baby wakes up, she won't be tired any more!"

Tell Them More of What's Happening in the World

There are many things we adults don't think of pointing out or explaining to children, but there's no reason not to. Children are extremely sensitive to changes in their environments or routines and are fascinated by things that don't work. When things go wrong, don't immediately set them right. Take the time to explain what happened. These unexpected incidents are built-in opportunities for language learning.

Things you could point out:

• new arrangement of furniture

• a new supply teacher

• a new toy

• a change in the weather

• a bird outside

• mud after the rain

Children are always interested in the misfortunes of others — like a teacher's sore finger.

Things you could explain:

• why you were absent from the centre

• why you got new furniture

• why the playdough is cold or hard

• why a toy doesn't work

• why the rabbit gets so little food to eat

Helping Children Become Better Story-tellers

Those of you working with toddlers, preschoolers and kindergartners are exposed to story-telling every day — not yours, but the children's. Narrative or story-telling is a very important skill which takes time to develop. While adults' stories can be extremely long and complicated, children's first stories may consist of just one word!

From these brief, immature accounts of events grow the ability to tell detailed, complex stories — stories that describe personal experiences or the experiences of others. Therefore, in this chapter, "story" refers to any account of an event or situation, not necessarily a story from a book.

The beginning of story-telling — what she's trying to say is "Gaby grabbed the book from me and broke it."

To tell a good story effectively, children must be able to:

- use vocabulary that is specific
- select the information which is relevant
- provide background information that the listener needs to know
- describe events and situations, using appropriate detail
- explain relationships between people and events, using conjunctions like "because," "but," and "when" and relative pronouns like "who," "that," and "which."
- describe the events in a logical sequence and make the story **interesting!**

The story-teller has to be aware of the listener's needs and background knowledge and has to adjust his use of language to accommodate these factors. If communication breaks down and the listener becomes confused, the story-teller has to judge what information he must provide to clear up the misunderstanding.

Good story-telling and descriptive skills are critical in both social and academic situations. Children need to be able to tell stories in order to participate fully in conversations and in dramatic play situations where stories are acted out. In addition, when children reach school age, their ability to recount experiences and tell stories will help them write and understand stories.

You can support and provide structure (scaffolds) for the child's story-telling by:

- asking questions that let the child know what information he needs to provide

- providing information upon which the child can build

Listen to how this teacher supports Dwayne, aged 4, in telling a story about his visit to the zoo:

Dwayne: *My Dad took me to the zoo and then he went home, and I stayed there all day.*

Teacher: *What do you mean your Dad went home? Didn't he go with you to the zoo?* (asks a question to clear up confusion)

Dwayne: *Well he drove me and my big cousin there, and then he left us there, and my cousin took me to see the animals.* (The teacher's question makes Dwayne realize that he needs to clarify his statement that his father "took" him to the zoo. He realizes that he needs to mention his cousin.)

Teacher: *Oh, I see. So you went to the zoo with your big cousin. And what did you see there?* (The teacher asks a scaffolding question, which helps the child continue the story.)

Dwayne: *We saw them spraying themselves with muddy water — they got so dirty and muddy!*

Teacher: **Who** *was spraying themselves with muddy water?* (Requests specific information.)

Dwayne: *The elephants — they were covered with mud. They really liked getting dirty.* (The teacher's question with the emphasis on "who" makes Dwayne realize that he hadn't mentioned which animal he was talking about.)

Teacher: *Wow! You were lucky to see that! Elephants do that to keep their skins cool. They don't like the heat.* (Provides interesting information on the topic, which, if he so chooses, the child can build on.)

After similar conversations, Dwayne will develop the ability to tell a story without needing as much support and guidance.

Plan to Encourage Story-telling

As teachers of young children, you have probably listened to many wild and wonderful stories. To become more aware of your role as a promoter of story-telling, ask yourself the following questions:

1. Do all the children in my room have opportunities to tell me stories

in relaxed, informal situations?

2. Do I make it possible for the quieter or less verbal children to tell me stories?

3. Do I listen well and give children time to finish their stories?

4. Do I model story-telling by telling children stories about my own experiences?

Here are some Do's for encouraging children's story-telling:

- **Do encourage story-telling in unstructured situations**
  e.g., during free play, sensory-creative activities, outdoor play and meal and snack time.

- **Do listen carefully to stories**
  Your facial expressions will show your interest — and will encourage the child to continue!

- **Do invite all children to tell stories**
  If one child in a group has just told a story, you could ask a quiet or less verbal child "Has anything like that ever happened to you?" or "What happened when you...?"

- **Do make leading statements that invite children to tell a story**
  e.g., "I'll bet you did something special during your holiday."

- **Do make comments that relate to the child's story**
  You can encourage children to continue their story with comments such as "That must have been so scary, getting lost in the supermarket!"

- **Do ask a sincere question to help the child continue with his story**

- **Do ask questions to make the child aware of information which is unclear or missing**

There's more than one positive way to respond to a story-teller

Here are some Don'ts for encouraging children's story-telling:

- **Don't make children's story-telling a large group activity**
  Circle time is not the best time to have each child tell a story — children will quickly get restless, and you'll lose your audience!

- **Don't interrupt or change the topic**
  Adults hate being interrupted — and so do children!

- **Don't turn the story into a "lesson" or "test"**
  If a child is telling you about his grandmother's new cat, don't ask "What do cats say?" or use this as an opportunity to teach the child about the cat family!

- **Don't forget to tell stories yourself!**

Summary

Children learn to talk and talk to learn during the conversations they have with their caregivers. Talking to learn involves using language to think and analyze, to problem-solve, to plan, to predict, to reason and to imagine, all of which provide the child with a solid foundation for all kinds of learning. Teachers can promote this "language of learning" by going beyond the here-and-now during their conversations with children, and by modelling these more abstract uses for language. They can also encourage and support children's storytelling, which demands specific, logically-sequenced, well-organized and descriptive use of language. By asking appropriate questions, making relevant comments and creating opportunities for all children to tell stories, teachers can promote this important skill.

References

Blank, M. (1973). *Teaching learning in the preschool: A dialogue approach.* Columbus, OH: Charles E. Merrill.

Blank, M. (1982). Language and school failure: Some speculations about the relationship between oral and written language. In L. Feagans and D.C. Farran (Eds.), *The language of children reared in poverty* (pp. 75-92). New York: Academic Press.

Crais, E.R. (1990). World knowledge to word knowledge. *Topics in Language Disorders, 10*(3), 45-62.

Farran, D.C. (1982). Mother-child interaction, language development and the school performance of poverty children. In L. Feagans and D.C. Farran (Eds.), *The language of children reared in poverty* (pp. 19-48). New York: Academic Press.

Graves, M. (1985). *A word is a word...or is it?* Richmond Hill, Ontario: Scholastic.

Heath, S.B. (1983). *Ways with words.* Cambridge, England: Cambridge University Press.

Heath, S.B. (1985). Separating "Things of the imagination" from life: Learning to read and write. In W.H. Teale & E. Sulzby (Eds.), (1985). *Emergent literacy: Writing and reading.* (pp. 156-172). Norwood, NJ: Ablex.

Lucariello, J. (1990). Freeing talk from the here-and-now: The role of event knowledge and maternal scaffolds. *Topics in Language Disorders, 10*(3), 14-29.

Shafer, R.E., Staab, C. & Smith, K. (1983). *Language functions and school success.* Glenview, IL: Scott, Foresman.

Snow, C.E., Dubber, C. & de Blauw, A. (1982). Routines in mother-child interaction. In L. Feagans and D.C. Farran (Eds.), *The language of children reared in poverty* (pp. 53-71). New York: Academic Press.

Tough, J. (1983). Children's use of language and learning to read. In L. Feagans and D.C. Farran (Eds.), *The language of children reared in poverty* (pp. 3-17). New York: Academic Press.

Tough, J. (1985). *Talking and learning.* Ward Lock Educational.

Umiker-Seboek, D.J. (1979). Preschool children's intraconversational narratives. *Journal of Child Language, 6,* 91-109.

Van Manen, M.(1986). *The tone of teaching.* Richmond Hill, Ontario: Scholastic.

Vygotsky, L. (1962). *Thought and language.* Cambridge: MIT Press.

Wallach, G.P. (1987). *Learning disabilities as a language problem: What to look for and what to do?* Presentation for the Toronto Association for Children with Learning Disabilities.

Warr-Leeper, G. (1992). *General suggestions for improving language.* Presentation at Clinical Symposium on "Current Approaches to the Management of Child Language Disorders" University of Western Ontario, London, Ontario.

Wells, G. (1986). *The meaning makers: Children learning language and using language to learn.* Portsmouth, New Hampshire: Heinemann.

Wells, J.L. (1980). *Children's language and learning.* Englewood Cliffs, NJ: Prentice Hall.

Wertsch, J.V. & Addison Stone, C. (1986). The concept of internalization in Vygotsky's account of the genesis of higher mental functions. In J. V. Wertsch (Ed.), *Culture, communication and cognition: Vygotskian perspectives* (pp.162-179). New York: Cambridge University Press.

Westby, C.E. (1985). Learning to talk — talking to learn: Oral-literate language differences. In C. Simon (Ed.), *Communication skills and classroom success* (pp. 181-218). San Diego: College Hill Press.

Yardley, A. (1988). *Discovering the physical world.* Toronto, Canada: Rubicon.

CHAPTER 9

Promote Pretend Play: Imagine the Fun, Imagine the Learning

232

A. Pretend Play: A Playful Context for Promoting Language Development

Teachers can encourage children to pretend and use their imaginations in many ways.

What separates humans from animals is humans' ability to use symbols. Your dog may be clever, but he can't talk, read or write! Humans use words as symbols, which makes it possible to represent the here-and-now, the past, the future and flights of fantasy. Your dog, however, has no way of letting you know that he enjoyed those cookies you left on the counter last night!

Pretend play, like language, involves the use of symbols, which is why it is also called symbolic play. During pretend play, pretend objects are used as symbols to represent absent objects. In time, children's ability to use symbols becomes so advanced that they no longer need objects; they can "act out" or use language to create make-believe.

Many experts believe that symbolic play is critical to a child's cognitive development. They believe it fosters abstract thought, problem-solving, self-control and creativity. The child's ability to use her imagination freely and creatively helps her in almost every aspect of life. As Albert Einstein said: "Imagination is more important than knowledge." And he knew!

Because pretend play and language reflect the same underlying cognitive capacity — i.e., the ability to represent things symbolically, children whose ability to use symbols is impaired (such as children with developmental delays) will have delays in both language and pretend play. Some children with language delays have immature pretend play skills due to their difficulty using symbols, but others may have excellent pretend play skills.

Because of the connection between language and pretend play, many experts believe that pretend play provides a rich context for language use, which helps children develop their language skills. Children who have strong symbolic play skills but poor language skills can be helped to develop language through pretend play, and children whose language skills seem more advanced than their symbolic play skills can be helped to use their language to pretend in more advanced ways. Pretend play offers all children wonderful opportunities for using and learning language in social situations.

Research has shown that if pretend play is not modelled and encouraged by caregivers, its development suffers. Therefore, it is important to encourage children to pretend and to use their imaginations in many ways. Some children won't need much encouragement to pretend and imagine, but those whose symbolic abilities are delayed or lacking will need much playful guidance.

B. The Development of Pretend Play

Children's pretend play develops in a predictable sequence from about 1 till 7 years of age, when it starts to fade. Children who have developmental delays and some children who have language delays take longer to reach these stages, and when they do reach them, they may not demonstrate the imaginativeness seen in their normally-developing peers.

Self-pretend Play (12 – 18 months)

- **the child plays at being herself**

Self-pretend play — the child pretends to go to sleep when he's not tired.

Are you pretending to sleep, Brian?

- **the child performs pretend actions on herself, using real-life objects or realistic-looking toys**
  She may pretend to drink from a cup or eat with a spoon.

Simple-Pretend Play (18 months – 2 years)

- **the child pretends by performing single actions on people or toys**
  The child is now able to perform pretend actions on others — e.g., she brushes a doll's hair or offers an adult a toy phone. She can also perform the same action on two different people, dolls or toys — e.g., she feeds herself with a spoon and then feeds a doll.

- **the child can substitute a toy object for the real object**
  The toy has to look similar to the "real thing" or the child won't be able to pretend with it.

- **the child pretends to do things she sees adults do**
  She may pick up a magazine and pretend to read it.

Sequence Pretend of Familiar Events and the Beginnings of Role Play (2 – 2½ years)

- **the child performs a sequence of several pretend actions in the appropriate order**
  The child's actions are drawn from familiar events — e.g., preparing and eating food, getting ready for bed, going out in a car.

- **the child begins to play the role of another person**
  The child role-plays someone she knows well (such as her mother), which indicates her developing awareness of others and her knowledge of how they should be represented during play. This is an important change in the child's ability to pretend.

Little children often play the role of "mother".

- **the child can now substitute one object for another**
  The substituted object must be **similar in shape** to the object for which it is being substituted — e.g., a stacking ring can represent a donut, but a block can't. At this stage, the child still needs objects that bear some resemblance to the real object to keep the make-believe going.

- **the child gives the doll a more active role in the play**
  Instead of performing actions only on the toy or doll, the child makes the doll perform actions for itself — e.g., she makes a bear hold a cup and drink from it.

Sequence Pretend of Less Familiar Events with Substitution of Dissimilar Objects (2½ – 3 years)

- **the child begins to act out less familiar events**
  The child may act out a trip to the doctor's office or pretend to be a hairdresser.

- **the pretending is action-based**
  The child acts out the event. She may talk while she plays, but talking is not an essential part of the pretense.

- **the child pretends with objects that don't look like the objects for which they stand**
  This development occurs at about 2½ years — e.g., the child pretends that a block is a car, puts a little man on the "car" and drives it to a "garage".

  This is an important achievement because the child can now represent the symbol's meaning in her mind without depending on the object's appearance. This means that her symbols are becoming separate from what they stand for, which is necessary for thinking, creating and problem-solving.

- **the child creates imaginary objects to support her play**
  The child may:

  — use mime or gesture to show what she is pretending to do — e.g., she may pat a pretend dog

  — use words and say "Here's my little dog!"

  — combine the two, and say "Here's my little dog!" and pretend to pat it.

  This "empty-handed miming" is an excellent indicator of the child's growing ability to create mental symbols without needing the support of objects.

  By 3 years of age, the child's ability to create mental symbols enables him to use imaginary objects in his play.

Sociodramatic Play: Planned Pretend Themes (3 – 5 years)

Pretend play is called dramatic play at this stage because it is like a dramatic performance. In sociodramatic play, a group of children collaborate in developing a theme within which they play the roles of people whom they would like to be. Sociodramatic play is person-oriented, not object-oriented, and is the most advanced form of pretend play.

Sociodramatic play has the following six elements:

- **role play**
  The children take on make-believe roles and either act them out or make a verbal statement about them — e.g., "I'm a doctor" — to let the group members know what their role is.

- **use of make-believe instead of realistic objects**
  The children create imaginary objects for their play by using gesture or mime and/or by stating what the imaginary object is — e.g., a child may say "Here's my scissors. I'm going to cut your hair" as she moves her two fingers apart and together, pretending to cut your hair. If objects are used, they frequently look nothing like the objects they are representing.

- **use of language to create make-believe actions or situations**
  The children use descriptions or make-believe statements to substitute for actions or situations — e.g., "Let's pretend that I'm the doctor and you've come to my hospital because your arm is broken."

- **extended play episodes**
  The children role-play or continue to act out a play theme for an extended period (at least 10 minutes), provided that enough time is provided.

- **interaction**
  At least two children interact and cooperate together in the play episode.

- **verbal communication**
  The children talk to one another about the play.

Changes in Sociodramatic Play with Age

Children at 3 years of age:	Children at 4 and 5 years of age:
• tend to act out themes of familiar events — e.g., playing house, cooking, feeding dolls etc.	• are very creative and inventive in their sociodramatic play and develop their own imaginary themes — e.g., kings and queens, monsters.
• are still dependent upon realistic props to get the play going, although they are able to pretend without them.	• enjoy using objects that are abstract and open-ended, like blocks and large boxes, for their play.
• engage in sociodramatic play for short periods of time because they are still learning how to negotiate and coordinate cooperative group play.	• can engage in sociodramatic play for long periods of time.
• may not be able to develop their dramatic play into a "story" with a plot, a sequence of events and an outcome.	• act out stories with a plot and play the roles of characters who come together to solve a problem or to produce some result.

The Importance of Language to Sociodramatic Play

In order to develop and play out a theme cooperatively and collaboratively during sociodramatic play, children need good verbal skills.

Language is used for 3 purposes during sociodramatic play:

i) To imitate people
ii) To establish and broaden the make-believe setting
iii) To coordinate and manage the play

i) To imitate people

When children engage in sociodramatic play, they are actually engaging in imitation; each child imitates a real person (like her mother or teacher) or one with whom she identifies (like a queen), trying to act, talk and look like that person. Through their play, children try to recreate a situation that is typical of the person whom they are imitating.

Children use language to imitate the person they are role-playing. For example, a child pretending to be a doctor might say "First I'm going to look in your mouth, then in your ears, and then I'll give you some medicine to make you better."

A child needs good language skills to imitate a real-life receptionist.

When would you like your next appointment, madam?

ii) To establish and broaden the make-believe setting

Of course, children can't actually reproduce a real-life situation; but they can create a make-believe one by using language to represent those things that can't actually be reproduced. They describe the make-believe setting to each other, interpret their actions so the other children understand their purpose and elaborate the play theme — by using language.

Language is used in four ways to establish and broaden the make-believe setting:

- **to take on a make-believe role**
  e.g., I'm the Mommy, you're the Daddy, and she can be the baby."

- **to establish the identity of objects**
  e.g., "This is my ice cream" (pretending to hold an ice cream cone).

- **to substitute for action**
  e.g., "Let's pretend that I already fed the baby and put her to bed" (these actions are only verbalized, not performed).

- **to plan and describe situations**
  e.g., "Let's pretend that we've got a million dollars and we're very rich."

Children need good language skills to plan their sociodramatic play.

I'll yell "**FIRE!**" and then you come and say, "**WHERE'S THE FIRE?**" and put it out.

iii) To coordinate and manage the play

There is no shortage of disagreements when children engage in sociodramatic play. But if they can't solve their problems, the play won't continue. Therefore, they use language to discuss their problems, to explain their points of view, to negotiate and to come up with creative solutions, as in the following example:

Brian: *I wanna be the father.*

Audrick: *You can't be the father because I'm the father.*

Brian: *How 'bout we both be fathers?*

Audrick: *You can't have two fathers. Nobody has two fathers.*

Brian: *Well, my cousin does. One lives with him and his mom, and the other one lives in a different house. He calls the one at his house "Frank" and the other one "Daddy".*

Audrick: *Okay then, but I want to be the one that's called Daddy.*

Brian: *Okay, I'll be Frank.*

Children learn and practise many language and conversational skills during sociodramatic play. They learn to follow the rules of conversation (as described in Chapter 4) and to see things from other children's points of view (as described in Chapter 6). Perhaps, as they assume the identity of another person, they are forced to consider what it must be like to be that person in order to play the role; this helps them appreciate the other person's perspective.

Children also learn to use clear, specific language during sociodramatic play — if they don't, confusion results. And research has shown that children who frequently engage in sociodramatic play have a better understanding of stories than those who don't.

Because there is so much to be gained from it, every child in your preschool and kindergarten classroom should engage in sociodramatic play.

C. Set the Stage for Pretend and Dramatic Play

To set the stage for pretend play and, in particular, for sociodramatic play, you need to provide five things:

- **Materials**
- **Time**
- **Space**
- **Models of playful pretend play**
- **Stimulating experiences**

Materials

Because children's play is heavily influenced by the available play materials, a great deal of attention should be paid to these materials.

Children who are less advanced in their pretend play prefer realistic-looking props. For these children, a house centre with toy dishes, pots, pans and recognizable food will stimulate pretend play.

Children whose dramatic play skills are more advanced will benefit from playing with objects that are open-ended. Blocks, boxes, milk cartons and paper-towel rolls present them with endless possibilities for using their imaginations. As they play with these open-ended materials, they are developing the ability to create symbols in their minds without being dependent on what the objects look like.

All the children are going to want to visit your zoo! Would you like to make some money out of this cardboard so they can pay to come and see the animals?

Yeah! We want to make lots of money!

They'll have to pay $5 to come in.

Interesting new props from the teacher help to enrich the play and keep it going!

A mixture of realistic and open-ended props will accommodate the children's varied levels of make-believe — and will provide something for everybody.

It is important to provide materials that encourage changes in theme in the dramatic play area. Materials that represent a store, an airplane, a doctor's office and a restaurant are just a few that children enjoy.

Time
Children need indoor free-play periods which are long enough for them to get really involved in their play. At least 30-50 minutes of uninterrupted play time is needed for this kind of play, and whenever possible, even longer periods should be provided.

Space
Your classroom needs a well-defined dramatic play area, even for toddlers. In addition, a block area, which also encourages pretend play, should be provided.

Models of playful pretend play
If children see that you value pretend play and are a playful pretender yourself, they will follow suit.

> *When children see you creatively model pretend play, they will be stimulated to create many imaginative ideas of their own.*

Seeing their teacher on all fours pretending to be "The Big Bad Wolf" encourages the children to become the "Three Little Pigs".

Stimulating Experiences

When children are familiar with the events about which they are pretending, their dramatic play is at its richest and can go on for extended periods. Playing "House" can last for half-an-hour, whereas playing "Astronauts" may last only five minutes because the children don't know enough about astronauts to keep the play going.

Parents who take their children to stores, to museums, to their workplaces and on outings are providing them with "raw material" for dramatic play. The content of these children's dramatic play will be far richer than that of children who haven't had these experiences.

You, too, can provide children with experiences that enrich their world knowledge. When field trips and special visitors to the centre are combined with discussion and enrichment through books and educational films, children gain a broader understanding of the adult world. Soon after, they will try out these ideas in their pretend play.

D. Observing Children's Pretend and Dramatic Play

When you observe children during free play activities, you learn a lot about their pretend play. When you are familiar with the development of pretend and dramatic play, as described in the first part of this chapter, you will become aware whether the child is:

- not pretending at all

- performing pretend actions only on herself

- performing pretend actions on others, single actions only

- performing sequences of pretend actions

- playing the role of another person

- substituting similar-looking objects for real objects

- substituting objects that don't resemble the real objects

- using imaginary objects

- role-playing themes alone

- role-playing themes with other children (sociodramatic play)

Before you can promote more mature forms of pretend play or use pretend play as a context for enhancing children's language skills, you must be familiar with the child's stage of pretend play.

E. Model Pretend Play for the Non-Pretender

Children who should be able to pretend but who don't, even when you "set the stage", need pretend play to be modelled for them.

Sherri, aged 2½, speaks in only one- or two-word sentences, but appears to understand far more than she can say. She is sitting on the floor, pushing the buttons on the toy phone but not pretending with it. Jan, her teacher, has been observing her for over a week and hasn't noted any pretend play at all.

1. **Jan observes that Sherri engages only in functional play — so she decides to model pretend play for her.**

2. **Jan pretends to talk to Sherri on the phone and offers her the other receiver to see if Sherri will imitate her.**

   Hello Sherri. How are you today?

3. **Sherri is imitating Jan's actions, saying nothing but showing an obvious interest in this game — which is a good beginning.**

   Should we call your Mommy at work and say, "Hi, Mommy! Hi! It's Sherri calling!"

Jan has both modelled pretend play for Sherri and treated her action of holding the phone to her ear **as if it were a pretend action**. By showing Sherri how an action with a toy object can symbolize a real-life action and by using language to clarify the meaning of her action, Jan is exposing Sherri to a model that, in time, she should be able to follow.

Jan will continue to model the use of pretend objects for Sherri in many situations. For example, she will invite Sherri to play in the house centre and will pretend to drink from a cup or eat some pretend food. If Sherri looks confused or looks for the water in the cup, for example, Jan will say "I'm pretending! See? I'm not really drinking. I'm just pretending," showing her the empty cup and "drinking" again.

F. Facilitate Sociodramatic Play

If preschoolers or kindergartners are able to pretend but can't use one or more of the elements of sociodramatic play, you can help them by modelling the missing elements.

> The six elements of sociodramatic play are:
> - **Role play**
> - **Use of make-believe instead of realistic objects**
> - **Use of language to create make-believe actions or situations**
> - **Extended play episodes (at least 10 minutes)**
> - **Interaction**
> - **Verbal communication**

In order to help children participate in and use the six elements of sociodramatic play, you can apply the following two techniques:

- **Outside Intervention: Providing Guidance Without Taking Part in the Play**

- **Inside Intervention: Providing Guidance While You Participate in the Play**

Outside Intervention: Providing Guidance Without Taking Part in the Play

In the same way that you can promote peer interaction without taking part in the play (see section on "Set Up Interactions from Outside the Group" in Chapter 6), so you can promote a child's participation in sociodramatic play by making comments and suggestions.

1. *Donna, who has a reluctant conversational style and engages only in solitary-dramatic play, needs help to get involved in the sociodramatic play in the "Supermarket". Joanne, her teacher, makes a suggestion designed to encourage Donna to take on the role of a parent, to use the doll as a make-believe child and to join in the children's play.*

2. *Joanne realizes that Donna is going to need some additional guidance in order to participate in the make-believe.*

3. *Sometimes Joanne makes a direct request of Donna to let her know how to participate in the play.*

When you provide outside intervention, you:

- don't need to take on a pretend role yourself

- talk to the children as if you were talking to the characters they are role-playing (so as not to disrupt the make-believe atmosphere)

- make suggestions that encourage the children to use sociodramatic play behaviours and interact with other children

Inside Intervention: Providing Guidance While You Participate in the Play

The goal of inside intervention is to help children develop all six elements of sociodramatic play and to fade yourself out as soon as they have done so. Inside intervention gives you the advantage of being able to model sociodramatic play behaviours that the children are not using while assuming a pretend role in the play yourself. This also makes it possible to support a number of children at the same time, as long as you know which element of the play you are trying to emphasize with each one.

You may need to play the director role in order to establish the theme and guide the play. However, it is important to do this in a gentle, playful manner which encourages the children to participate.

Inside Intervention: An Example

Gill is going to play with Petra, Craig and Nicki

Petra *still depends on realistic objects for her play and so, for her, Gill needs to model the use of make-believe instead of realistic objects.*

Craig *uses all six elements of sociodramatic play, and so he is a good model for the other two children.*

Nicki *engages in action-based pretend play, but not in any kind of dramatic play. Gill wants to model dramatic role-play for her and show her how language can be used to role-play a character and to create a make-believe situation.*

1. Gill starts the "hairdresser" theme off with an invitation that no one can refuse.

2. Gill invites Petra to wash her hair, which involves spraying make-believe water onto her head. Craig's offer of a cup as the shampoo bottle shows Petra how objects can be used for make-believe even if they look nothing like the real-life object. And now Nicki is really interested!

3. Gill prepares Nicki for the role she will play when Petra has finished "washing" her hair. When Petra rejects the use of a blanket as a towel, Gill shows her how you can transform any object by making a statement about what you want it to be.

> Could you hold this towel ready so you can dry my hair when Petra is finished?

> That's not a towel. That's a dolly blanket.

> Let's pretend that it **is** a towel.

> I've got my scissors and I'm ready to cut your hair.

> My hair's nearly dry. Nicki's just drying it a little more.

4. Nicki, who is having a lot of fun, is actively contributing to the play. She is being exposed to language that is used to imitate real-life characters, to establish the make-believe situation and to manage the play.

> Let me look in my mirror. Wow, my hair looks great! And it feels so clean!

5. After one last look in Gill's imaginary mirror, she and the children are delighted with the results!

Children may respond slowly to your efforts to introduce them to the elements of sociodramatic play. However, as soon as they demonstrate all six elements of sociodramatic play, you can withdraw and let them gain confidence in their ability to play independently. Or you can stay — but make sure you follow their lead.

G. Join In and Add to the Children's Sociodramatic Play

Children with well-developed sociodramatic play skills don't need you to direct their play, but they will enjoy it when, from time to time, you join in, assume a make-believe role and follow their lead. While doing this, you will have many opportunities to:

- model play behaviours that expand the play

- encourage more conversation within pretend roles

- add ideas that will enrich the children's understanding of the theme

1. The children are playing "Restaurant".

2. Leslie joins in by pretending to be a customer.

3. Leslie is invited to join the group, and she does. Since the children are role-playing adults in a real-life restaurant, Leslie models real-life adult conversation and requests a menu, which expands the play.

4. Leslie's true-to-life imitation of a customer in a restaurant helps the children enrich their play.

5. Leslie models the kind of language adults really use in restaurants, thereby encouraging more mature language and more play-related conversation.

H. Encourage Pretend Play During Sensory-Creative Activities

Because sensory-creative activities are so open-ended, they have great potential for fostering pretend and dramatic play. Children often let you know that they are ready to pretend, but if you don't respond to their cues, the play won't take off.

Manny is ready to pretend, but his teacher is stuck in the here-and-now.

Look at how much more fun they have when the teacher follows Manny's lead and expands on the make-believe.

Summary

Pretend play is an important part of children's lives; it fosters cognitive development and provides an excellent context for language development. Sociodramatic play, which involves the collaborative role play of themes by a group of children, is the most advanced form of pretend play and has a significant impact on children's social and language skills. In child care settings, teachers need to set the stage for pretend play by providing space, materials, adequate time to play, stimulating experiences and a playful model. Teachers can encourage the development of pretend play by modelling it for children who seem unable to pretend and by guiding participation in sociodramatic play with comments, suggestions, models of the missing elements and creative ideas for expanding the play's theme.

References

Bretherton, I. (1984). Representing the social world in symbolic play: Reality and fantasy. In I. Bretherton (Ed.), *Symbolic Play: The development of social understanding* (pp. 3-41). New York: Academic Press.

Bretherton, I. (1986). Representing the social world in symbolic play: Reality and fantasy. In Gottfried, A.W. and C. Caldwell Brown (Eds.), *Play interactions: The contribution of play materials and parental involvement to children's development*. Proceedings of the eleventh Johnson and Johnson Pediatric Round Table (pp.119-148). Lexington, Mass: Lexington Books.

Christie, J.F. & Wardle, F. (1992). How much time is needed for play? *Young Children, 47*(3), 28-31.

Copple, C., Sigel, I.E. & Saunders, R. (1984). *Educating the young thinker: Classroom strategies for cognitive growth.* Hillsdale, NJ: Lawrence Erlbaum Associates.

Fenson, L. (1986). The developmental progression of play. In Gottfried, A.W. and C. Caldwell Brown (Eds.), *Play interactions: The contribution of play materials and parental involvement to children's development.* Proceedings of the eleventh Johnson and Johnson Pediatric Round Table (pp.53-65). Lexington, Mass: Lexington Books.

Garvey, C. (1990). *Play.* Cambridge, Mass: Harvard University Press.

Johnson, J.E., Christie, J.F. & Yawkey, T.D. (1987). *Play and early childhood development.* Glenview, IL: Scott, Foresman.

McCune, L. (1986). Play-language relationships: Implications for a theory of symbolic development. In Gottfried, A.W. and C. Caldwell Brown (Eds.), *Play interactions: The contribution of play materials and parental involvement to children's development.* Proceedings of the eleventh Johnson and Johnson Pediatric Round Table (pp.67-79). Lexington, Mass: Lexington Books.

McCune-Nicolich, L. (1981). Towards symbolic functioning: Structure of early pretend games and potential parallels with language. *Child Development, 52,* 785-797.

Nelson, K. & Seidman, S. (1984). Playing with scripts. In I. Bretherton (Ed.), *Symbolic Play: The development of social understanding* (pp. 3-41). New York: Academic Press.

Paley, V. (1990). *The boy who would be a helicopter.* Cambridge, Mass: Harvard University Press.

Pellegrini, A.D. (1985). Relations between preschool children's symbolic play and literate behaviour. In L. Galda and A.D. Pellegrini (Eds.), *Play, language and stories: The development of children's literate behaviour* (pp. 79-97). Norwood, NJ: Ablex.

Pellegrini, A.D. & Galda, L. (1990). Children's play, language and early literacy. *Topics in Language Disorders, 10*(3), 76-88.

Segal, M. & Adcock, D. (1981). *Just pretending: Ways to help children grow through imaginative play.* Englewood Cliffs, NJ: Prentice Hall.

Smilansky, S. & Shefatya, L. (1990). *Facilitating play: A medium for promoting cognitive, socio-emotional and academic development in young children.* Gaithersburg, MD: Psychosocial and Educational Publications.

Weininger, O. (1988). "What if" and "As if': Imagination and pretend play in early childhood. In K. Egan and D. Nadaner (Eds.), *Imagination and Education* (pp.141-149). New York: Teachers College Press.

Westby, C. (1980). Language abilities through play. *Language, Speech, and Hearing in the Schools, 11,* 154-168.

Wetherby, A. (1991a). *Profiling communication and symbolic abilities: Assessment and intervention guidelines.* Presentation at Toronto Children's Centre, Toronto, Ontario.

Wetherby, A. (1991b). Profiling pragmatic abilities in the emerging language of young children. In T, M. Gallagher, (Ed.), *Pragmatics of language: Clinical practice issues* (pp. 249-281). San Diego, CA: Singular.

PART 4

LET LANGUAGE LEAD THE WAY TO LITERACY

Children learn about literacy from birth, and they learn about it much the same way as they learn about spoken language.

As they interact with their caregivers in natural day-to-day situations, they see them use print in meaningful ways and they discover that those marks on paper actually mean something. And once they discover that print communicates, they want to know — **how?**

As a teacher, you play an important role in helping children develop the attitudes, skills and knowledge that lead to literacy.

Children must be helped to discover:

> **What I do or see or hear or touch, I can talk about**
>
> **What I talk about, I can write about, or someone can write for me**
>
> **What is written down, I can read or someone can read for me**

In this approach to literacy, better known as the Whole Language approach, children develop reading and writing as they participate in meaningful literacy events. This approach can benefit all children, including children with language delays who have the same need to be involved in purposeful and relevant literacy-related activities as their peers.

Chapter 10, "Pave the Way for Young Readers and Writers", provides in-depth information on how teachers can lay the foundations of literacy by making reading and writing a natural, meaningful part of every day.

In Chapter 11, "Circle Time: An Interactive Language-learning Experience", you will read about stimulating and interactive circles that build the language skills which children need in order to become literate.

CHAPTER 10

Pave the Way for Young Readers and Writers

A. Laying the Foundations of Literacy

There was a time when early literacy began with teaching children the alphabet. Not any more. Children have many more important things to learn about spoken language, reading and writing before they are ready to understand the purpose of the alphabet.

Children need to:

- **Develop positive attitudes toward the use of print**
- **Build their background knowledge and language skills**
- **"Play" with words**
- **Develop an awareness of print**

Helping Children Develop Positive Attitudes Toward the Use of Print

The attitudes which children develop toward reading and writing and which they bring to the task of developing literacy, are so important. In order to become competent readers and writers, children must **want** to read and write. Positive attitudes toward reading and writing are passed on to children from their parents and caregivers. Children of actors, singers and tennis players often want to be actors, singers and tennis players. Children whose parents frequently read and write also want to be readers and writers.

As a teacher, you send strong messages to children (even to infants and toddlers) about how important reading and writing are to you. So let the children see your positive attitude toward reading and writing.

This was my favourite book when I was little!

When you get excited about books, so do the children.

What you can do:

- Get really excited about books
- Talk about the books you read
- Show the children the books that were your childhood favourites
- Bring in interesting pictures or articles from newspapers and magazines
- Let the children see that writing is a natural part of your day

More of these ideas will be discussed later in this chapter.

The Importance of Background Knowledge and Language Skills to Reading

Good language skills, a wide vocabulary and a well-developed store of background knowledge are essential for a child to become a successful reader.

Read the story below and see how you use your language skills, vocabulary and background knowledge to fill in what's missing.

Miranda's Miserable Day

Miranda was late for the important staff meeting. She couldn't afford to lose her (i)_____ and she knew that if she missed this meeting, there was a good chance that she (ii)_____. She locked (iii)_____ door of her apartment and rushed outside. She tried to hail a (iv)_____, but her efforts were entirely unsuccessful. Finally, she decided to take the (v) b_____, which resulted in her arriving at her office 20 minutes late. She (vi) <u>draimed</u> up the stairs and into the meeting room, where she was met by a stony-faced Mr. Crimp, who said, (vii) "_____ _____!"

Look at what your language skills and knowledge of the topic enabled you to do:

1. **You probably figured out what the story was about from the title "Miranda's Miserable Day" and from the first sentence: "Miranda was late for the important staff meeting".**
   The title and the words "late" and "meeting" gave you the idea that the story was about Miranda's problems at work. You were able to reach this conclusion fairly easily because you are familiar with this theme from reading novels, watching movies and perhaps from personal experience. Your ability to use language enabled you to make these assumptions and reach this conclusion.

   Children, too, must learn to make assumptions and reach conclusions about what they read. Their ability to use language to think, problem-solve and reason enables them to understand things not specifically mentioned in the story. For example, if a child with good language skills read the sentence "He ran into his room, reached for the switch and immediately began searching for the ring", he would immediately make a number of inferences: it was night time (because he reached for the switch), he switched on the light (so he could look for the ring) and the ring was lost (because he was searching for it).

   Because authors never include every detail in their stories, children have to reach many conclusions on their own. If they are unable to use language to draw these conclusions, they are likely to miss the meaning of the story and become frustrated. Therefore, the ability to problem-solve and look for connections and possible explanations, which is an important part of the language of learning, is critical to becoming an effective reader.

Having a broad general knowledge helps children make these assumptions. If they are read to regularly, they develop this knowledge, and they draw upon it when they listen to and read stories. In the same way that your exposure to the topic of "Problems at Work" helped you figure out what Miranda's story was about, so children who have heard stories and read books about detectives, jungle animals, dinosaurs or birds of prey will find it easier to understand books on these topics.

2. You knew that the missing word for number (i) ("She couldn't afford to lose her _____ ") was "job" and for number (iv) ("She tried to hail a _____,") was "cab" or "taxi."
Your knowledge of language helped you decide what would make sense in these sentences. Within the theme "Problems at Work", you would expect "lose her...." to be followed by "**job**," as opposed to an umbrella or a set of keys. In addition, the expression **"hail a..."** is usually followed by "cab" or "taxi," and in the context of trying to get somewhere fast, it wasn't difficult to reach this conclusion.

Children with well-developed language skills also use their "feel" for language to help them anticipate what word comes next in a sentence. They learn vocabulary and common expressions during conversations with adults as well as from regular exposure to books.

3. Your knowledge of English grammar told you that the missing word for number (ii) ("...and she knew that if she missed this meeting, there was a good chance that she _____.") was "would" and for number (iii) ("She locked _____ door of her apartment and rushed outside.") was "the".
If English is your first language, your instinctive knowledge of the rules of English grammar makes these answers obvious. This task is more difficult for people who speak English as a second language and have not learned all the rules of English grammar.

When children learn to read, their instinctive knowledge of grammatical rules helps them figure out unknown words in the same way your instinctive knowledge of rules helped you in the examples above. From the position of the word in the sentence and from the words that come before and after the unknown word, children gain important clues. For example, if a child couldn't read the word "flung" in the sentence "He flung the bag into the air", he would, without realizing it, still know a lot about the word; he would know that the word "flung" was a verb because it came after the subject of the sentence. Because the subject of the sentence was a person and not an object, he would know that the verb probably involved an action of some sort on the bag. All this makes it easier to figure out the meaning of the word.

Children with immature or delayed language often have trouble learning to read, partly because books contain grammatical rules which they haven't yet grasped. This also affects second language learners.

*For example, if a child isn't able to use the passive tense, such as "The dog **was bitten** by the bird," he is unlikely to understand such a sentence. Therefore, he will interpret the sentence as "The dog bit the bird," which destroys the meaning of the story. These children need to be helped to learn grammatical rules (see Chapter 7) and need a great deal of exposure to books that they can enjoy and understand.*

4. **Your knowledge of phonics and spelling made it obvious that number (v) ("Finally, she decided to take the b_____, which resulted in her arriving at her office 20 minutes late.") had to be "bus."**
   If the letter "b" hadn't been there, the word could have been "train," "streetcar" or "subway," but the "b" made the choice obvious. In this way, you used your knowledge of phonics to work out what would make sense.

   As children learn letter-sound relationships (phonics), they use this knowledge to help them narrow down the possibilities when reading an unknown word. However, knowledge of phonics is not enough to help them understand what they are reading (see No. 6. below for discussion of the meaning of "draimed").

5. **Exposure to "the language of books" helped you understand the phrase "but her efforts were entirely unsuccessful."**
   Even though most of us don't talk like this, we have read enough books for these kinds of expressions to be part of our receptive vocabularies.

   Children who have been frequently read to become familiar with the language of books, which helps them comprehend more complex language.

6. **You have a good idea of what "draimed" means in the sentence "She <u>draimed</u> up the stairs and into the meeting room" even though you've never seen the word before!**
   There is no such word as "draimed"! But you knew what would make sense in that context and concluded that "draimed" meant something like "rushed", "charged" or "dashed". Because we constantly search for meaning in what we read, we do this kind of "educated guessing" frequently and we become quite good at it.

   Because children come across many, many words that they don't know when they learn to read, they must be encouraged to make educated guesses at them. "Sounding out" the word doesn't always help; words that are easy to "sound out" may still mean nothing to a child. For example, words like "mist," "snub" and "tot" aren't hard words to read, but they aren't part of most children's vocabulary. And while sounding out words can be useful, if that's the only strategy children use, they often lose the meaning of what they read. Children who are encouraged to work out what would "make sense" in a particular context become readers who always try to understand what they read — and after all, that's what reading is about.

7. You probably guessed that the stony-faced Mr. Crimp said "You're fired!" or "You're late!" for number (vii).

Your sense of story, gained from reading many stories and from watching movies, enabled you to **predict** what Mr. Crimp was likely to say. This is a critical skill for readers to develop. Predicting gives readers an expectation about what will happen next, which is part of the reader's ongoing effort to interact with and understand the story. Predicting what will happen next makes reading more meaningful and more interesting (especially if your prediction isn't right, which is why many people love good mysteries).

Children who have had many stories read to them and who are encouraged to predict during story reading become good predictors.

8. You imagined this scene in your head.

As you read the story, you were able to use the words to help you create an image of this scene in your mind. You could picture Miranda, her desperation and the miserable Mr. Crimp. Your ability to understand language and to use it to go beyond the real world enabled you to imagine something you had never experienced.

Children with excellent language skills and vivid imaginations find it easier to interpret what they read; it is possible that their ability to use symbols helps them transform verbal descriptions into mental images.

As you can see from this exercise, what enables a child to become a successful reader are his language skills — his knowledge of grammar, his ability to use the language of learning and his familiarity with the language of books. He must grasp the rules of grammar or he will have difficulty reading sentences that contain grammar more complex than his own. As he reads a story, he must also be able to use language to explain, predict, project and imagine, constantly analyzing what he reads, deciding what it means, imagining the scene in his mind and correcting his predictions or assumptions when they are proved to be wrong. He must also become familiar with the language of books, which is more complex and formal than spoken language.

> **What you can do:**
>
> - Encourage and model the language of learning for the children during your everyday conversations with them (as described in Chapter 8)
>
> - Expose the children to many, many books so they learn to go beyond the here-and-now, so they gain exposure to the language of books and develop a broad general knowledge
>
> - Encourage the children to figure out what words mean
>
> - Encourage the children to think about a story — to predict, imagine and project
>
> - Encourage the children to make sense of the book by relating it to what they already know

These suggestions will be discussed in more detail later in the chapter.

"Playing" with Words: An Important Game

Children need to learn that language is made up of many different parts, that sentences can be broken up into words and that words can be broken up into syllables and sounds. They must also become aware of the rules that dictate how all the parts of language go together (this includes grammatical rules, described in Chapter 7).

The process of "thinking about language" starts early in life. Even infants show signs of this when they "repair" a breakdown in communication by changing the way they send their messages. When a 3-year-old says "Pumpernickel" twenty times, giggling uncontrollably because the word has such a funny sound, he's actually thinking about language and, better still, he's **playing** with it!

Listen to 3- and 4-year-olds as they:

- **change the words of rhymes and songs**
  e.g., "Nathan the red-nosed reindeer, Had a very shiny nose..." (Nathan, aged 4, was not impressed)

- **make up funny-sounding words**
  e.g., "Your name will be Mr. Boodleboodle!" (Hysterical laughter)

- **change the sounds in words**
  e.g., "I'm eating a nabana." (banana)

- **make up rhyming words**
  e.g., "You're Jake the snake," "And you're Matt the bat."

- **play with word meanings**
  e.g., "In winter, a somersault should be called a wintersault."
  (amazing for a 4-year-old)

- **say phrases or lists of words that sound alike**
  e.g., "Big baby boy, big baby boy... those all sound the same."

- **recognize pronunciation errors**
  e.g., "He says 'top' instead of 'stop.'"

These children are already aware how words and sentences can be broken up and put back together again. Children who can "play" with language like this will find reading, writing and spelling easier to learn.

Teachers who prepare young children for reading by teaching them "'c'-is-for-cat" kinds of phonic skills are way ahead of schedule. Young children need to "play" with language in the ways described above before they are ready to learn how words can be broken down into individual sounds. This is especially important for children with language delays whose ability to "play with words" is often below age level.

What you can do:

- Follow the children's lead when they play with words! And add your own ideas.

- Play with words yourself
  e.g., "See ya later alligator; in the house, little mouse; on a chair, big brown _____."

- Make up new songs to old tunes

- Sing songs whose verses can be changed to make many different rhymes

e.g., There was Shane, Shane,	There was Mark, Mark,
Dancing in the rain,	Sleeping in the dark,
In the store,	In the store,
In the store...	In the store...

- Point out interesting things about words or names
  e.g., "Hey! Ryan and Rob both have names that start with 'r'!"

  "My name is so loooong. Listen to how many parts it has — Chris-ti-na. Three parts!" (as you tap once for each syllable.)

  Do this playfully and informally — that's why it's called playing with words!

Developing an Awareness of Print

From an early age, children become aware of the print they see, and they try to figure out what it means. This marks the beginning of reading.

By 3 years of age, many children can read signs in the environment such as "EXIT," "STOP" or "MacDonalds" (of course!). From being read to, they have learned where the book begins, in which direction to turn the pages and that it is the print and not the pictures that tells the story. They know that the story continues from page to page, and they use words like "read," "story" and "page" appropriately.

Children know that writing involves making marks on paper, and their earliest attempts at writing involve scribbling. Scribbling is an important part of learning to write and shows a definite progression from random scribbles to controlled scribbles to naming of scribbles.

In time, children come to realize that writing is organized in lines and they also develop a sense of what letters should look like. As a result, their scribbles become repetitive and go across the page, and the children enjoy "reading" what they have "written". Before too long, they start to write mock letters and words and finally, they progress to writing real letters and words (especially their names). They experiment in many ways, writing what they know again and again, copying words in the environment and eventually learning to write from left to right.

This is a process of discovery, and you can encourage this process in a natural way.

Scribbling and experimenting with "letter-like"
forms are important parts of learning to write.

> **What you can do:**
>
> - Point out print in the environment and in books: first words in a story, strange-looking words, long words, short words, unusual print — e.g., "BOOM!", labels on boxes, signs etc.
>
> - Provide many opportunities for drawing and scribbling with crayons, markers, pencils, fingerpaint etc.
>
> - Encourage children to write in their own way for many different purposes — e.g., to label their pictures, to write to their friends, parents etc.
>
> - Don't worry about correct spelling or perfect letter formation; writing, like talking, improves with exposure and experience. Correcting spelling and letter formation too early distracts children from the purpose of writing, which is to communicate.
>
> - Provide help with printing, spelling or writing stories only when asked.
>
> - Let the children know that you consider their writing to have meaning. Respond to what they want their writing to "say".

This will be discussed in more detail later in the chapter.

B. Book-reading: A Time for Sharing and Learning

Books connect children with the world — their own world and new worlds. The illustrations and stories transport them into situations which expand their knowledge, experience and imagination. Their fascination with books will bring them back to their favourite books again and again.

It's never too early to enjoy books.

Book reading has an advantage over conversation: the language in books doesn't "disappear" as the language of conversation does — it comes back each time the book is read. As the children hear the stories again and again, they understand more about the book, and its language becomes familiar. It becomes so predictable that eventually the child takes over and "reads" the book himself. This is one of the best ways to encourage children to read independently; when they know the book well, they feel as if they can read it. Eventually, they will be right.

It is through reading books (and especially reading the same book again and again) that much language learning takes place. By listening to stories and by discussing them with an interested adult, children develop a store of knowledge about the world and come to understand words and concepts that they could not learn as easily from casual conversation. For this reason, children who have language delays can benefit a great deal from being read to, particularly in small groups or on an individual basis.

So when you hear a child talk about a Tyrannosaurus Rex or use a phrase such as "to the very top" or "once and for all" which he heard in a book, you can be sure that he has begun that all-important journey into the language of books.

Don't Just Read the Book!

Reading aloud to children isn't just an activity — it's a performance and you're the performer! As the reader, you have to draw your listeners into the story by creating the right mood, and you have to be aware of your audience's reaction and adapt accordingly. Whether you are reading informally to one or two children or to a larger group of children at circle time, the interaction between you and your listeners is the key to success.

This teacher is just reading...

So give it all you've got — be dramatic, animated and look excited. Add different voices for different characters and use sound effects for noises in the book. Get the children involved and keep them involved!

...but this teacher is animated and expressive, and she's captured the children's attention.

Read the Right Books

All children's books are not created equal. Some are excellent, some are mediocre and some are dreadful! If the children become restless during book-reading, consider whether the fault lies with the book; it may be too simple or be simply too boring!

In deciding which books to read to the children, there is one important guideline:

Children should be exposed only to the best books!

Reading to children is important in laying the foundation for them to become readers, but it's not enough to turn them into enthusiastic readers. Books which enchant, amuse, move and delight children inspire them to become readers. Therefore, choose books carefully, bearing in mind the children's interests and stage of language development. (Remember that children's ability to appreciate a book depends on what they can **understand**, not what they can say.) Because the children "read" the illustrations while you read the book, the book's illustrations should be interesting to look at, clear and quite large, and they should correspond with the book's content.

> *Reading to children is important in laying the foundation for them to become readers, but it's not enough to turn them into enthusiastic readers. Books which enchant, amuse, move and delight children inspire them to become readers.*

If the children aren't paying attention, you may be reading the wrong book.

C. Exposing Children to Books at Stages 1, 2 and 3

Before children understand that pictures in books represent real objects and people, they tend to enjoy chewing them. Trying to "read" the book to a child at these early stages of language development usually results in his pulling the book away from you and putting it straight back in his mouth!

The first thing babies do with books is eat them!

Cardboard books with good, clear illustrations and books containing collections of nursery rhymes are best for very young infants. Perhaps they can eat the cardboard books while they enjoy listening to the rhythm and sound of the nursery rhymes!

D. Building on Children's Fascination with Books at Stage 4

Children at this stage of language development have started to use words (the beginning of symbol use), and they realize that pictures in books represent real people and objects (pictures are symbols too). As a result, they become fascinated with books.

Choosing the Best Books for Children at Stage 4

Some of the best books for children at Stage 4 are:

— Mother Goose collections

— Board books with pictures that encourage the labelling and pointing that is typical of children at this stage of language development

— Song books (books with illustrated songs)

— Family photograph albums

— Interaction books — e.g., "Pat the Bunny."

The book should:

- appeal to the children's interests and level of understanding

- have clear, colourful and appealing illustrations

- have only a small amount of print on each page

- be short

- be easy to manipulate

Guidelines for Reading with Children at Stage 4

There's a lot of language that children at this stage can't understand, and so you have to help them make sense of the book. This means that **you can't always read the book exactly as it's written!** In the same way that you adjust your language when you are talking to children to help them understand you, so you need to adjust the way you read books to them.

- **Give the child information he can understand**
  Use clear, simple language to describe the picture to the child. (The text in the book may give too much information or not enough.)

A simple, clear sentence helps the child understand what's in the book.

The mommy is on the phone.

- **Clarify your meaning by:**

  — repeating and exaggerating key words

  — using gestures or pantomime

  — using "fun" words — e.g. "Boom!"

  — showing props or real objects that are similar to the pictures in the book

  — comparing or contrasting the information with something in the immediate environment

  — providing a simple explanation

Pantomime helps children understand what the words in the book mean.

Use props to reinforce what you have shown the child in the book.

- **Observe the children's reactions to the book**
  Much of the learning that takes place during book-reading occurs as the children interact with you and communicate about the book. If possible, seat the child or children so you can see their faces and pick up their initiations. Because most young children love to sit on your lap when being read to (often two at a time), try seating them at a slight angle so you can see whether they are staring intently at an illustration or pointing at something.

- **Wait — and don't rush the reading**
  Pace your reading according to the children's interests and give them time to look at each page (often they will be fascinated by one page in particular). When you do, you will encourage them to initiate.

- **Listen**
  If you listen closely, you may find that a very quiet child has a lot to say (even if the sounds aren't real words).

- **Follow the Child's Lead**
  Respond to the children's initiations by labelling, interpreting and commenting — and have a little conversation. Children at this stage often point to pictures and want you to label them. And they enjoy it when you ask them to label pictures whose names they know. From these interactions, children learn that books are fun to talk about.

E. Using Books to Stimulate and Satisfy Children's Curiosity at Stage 5

At this stage children are incredibly curious, and books provide them with a wonderful source of stimulation to which they can return at any time. Now that their receptive language has increased, they can enjoy a wider variety of books.

Choosing the Best Books for Children at Stage 5

Some of the best books for children at Stage 5 are:

— Books with collections of pictures — e.g., Richard Scarry books.

— Books with a repetitive theme and "fun-sounding" words — e.g., "Hand, Hand, Fingers, Thumb" by Al Perkins.

— Theme books on topics such as zoo animals, babies, toys, "Things I can do myself," etc.

— Short stories with a very simple plot and story line — e.g., "Just for You" and "Just a Mess" by Mercer Mayer.

— Classics — e.g., "Goodnight Moon" by Margaret Wise Brown.

— Stories which are repetitive and predictable — e.g., "The Ginger-bread Man".

— Collections of poems and nursery rhymes.

— Participatory books — e.g., "Pat the Bunny" and "Where's Spot?"

Guidelines for Reading with Children at Stage 5

• **Respond to the children's initiations**
Build on the child's interest and respond to his initiations by confirming and expanding on them.

Children's initiations during book-reading provide you with many opportunities to expand on their message.

Sometimes I find something interesting.

• **Rephrase the text when necessary**
Some books have wonderful illustrations but poor text. Consider whether the text relates to the illustration in a way the children can understand; if not, you'll need to rephrase it.

There's no mention of the word "shoe"; you'll need to rephrase the text.

• **Let the children join in!**
No child can resist the appeal of "Who's been sleeping in **my** bed?" or "Run, run as fast as you can, you can't catch me, I'm the Gingerbread Man!" These stories are fun to listen to, and they have children anxiously waiting to chime in! As children wait for the opportunity to yell out the word or words that complete the sentence, they are learning to predict what comes next which, as discussed in "Miranda's Miserable Day", is an important reading skill.

Once the children are familiar with a predictable story, give them a chance to chime in by stopping and waiting expectantly at the appropriate spot in the story.

...And the daddy bear said, " Who's been sleeping in my bed?" And the mommy bear said, " Who's been sleeping in my ... "

BED!

• **Bring the book to life**
When you relate the content of the book to something the children already know and when you provide opportunities for them to interact with the story, you bring the book to life.

For example, if you were reading "The Gingerbread Man," you could bring in real gingerbread men for the children to eat. Or, once they were familiar with the story, you could give each child a cardboard gingerbread man and have them "act out" the story as you read it.

F. Encouraging the "Language of Learning" when Reading with Children at Stages 6 and 7

Language has opened up the world to children at this stage. They can go beyond the here-and-now, beyond their own personal experience and beyond the real world into the world of make-believe, and books enable them to do just that. They have developed the "language of learning" (see Chapter 8), which they use to think about and understand the book in the same way you did when reading "Miranda's Miserable Day".

Children at this stage can understand and appreciate both fiction and non-fiction. However, there is still a very wide range of abilities and interests between the ages of 3 and 5, and the books to which you expose children must still be chosen carefully.

Choosing the Best Books for Children at Stages 6 and 7

- **The book's topic or story line should appeal to the children's interests and level of understanding.**
  As children develop more advanced receptive language skills, they enjoy and understand stories with more complex plots and imaginary themes.

  4- and 5-year-olds, who engage in imaginative dramatic and sociodramatic play are well able to appreciate books about fantasy, such as "Where the Wild Things Are" by Maurice Sendak and "Miss Nelson is Missing" by Harry Allard. Children who can recognize their own feelings and fears will love books like "There's a Nightmare in my Closet" by Mercer Mayer and "I Have to Go" by Robert Munch.

- **Provide books with excellent language**
  Descriptions such as *"...and he sailed off through night and day and in and out of weeks..."* (from Maurice Sendak's "Where the Wild Things Are") cannot but enchant children at the same time as they expose them to imaginative ways of using language.

  Let the children hear language that has a more sophisticated style, grammatical structure and vocabulary. The beauty of the words *"The wild things roared their terrible roars and gnashed their terrible teeth..."* combines a wonderful use of repetition and rhythm with new vocabulary which children respond to and remember.

- **Read more detailed and complex stories**
  Children develop story structure or a "sense of story" from having many stories read to them. Story structure, which will be illustrated by the fairy tale "The Three Little Pigs," consists of the following basic parts:

  — introduction of the setting and the main characters
    The three pigs and the big bad wolf

— an event or problem which leads you into the story
The wolf huffs and puffs and blows down two pigs' houses

— a response from the main characters or an attempt to deal with the problem
The third pig builds a strong house, saves his brothers and puts a kettle of boiling water at the bottom of the chimney

— outcome of the attempt
The wolf falls into the boiling water and dies

— reaction from main characters
The three pigs live happily ever after

Fairy tales have a very well-defined story structure which helps children develop a sense of story, making it easier for them to follow the story and predict what will happen next.

Guidelines for Reading Books with Children at Stages 6 and 7

Before you read the book:
- Preview the book
- Read the book's title, show the children the cover and encourage them to predict what the book is about
- Introduce the author and illustrator
- Create a purpose for reading the book

While you are reading the book:
- Take some time to respond to questions and comments
- Wonder aloud about what might happen next
- Stimulate the children to think about the story, using the "language of learning"
- Explain things the children don't understand

After reading the book:
- Encourage the children's spontaneous comments
- Help the children make connections between this and other books
- Offer some interesting follow-up activities
- Encourage the children to "read" the book themselves

After much experience with story reading, children can appreciate stories which are more detailed and complex. In time, they will enjoy stories that have more complicated "problems", more than one attempt to solve the problem (including some failed attempts) and less obvious outcomes.

- **Provide a mixture of non-fiction and fiction**
  Satisfy the children's all-encompassing curiosity by reading them books on topics such as dinosaurs, snakes, sharks, animals and their young and the solar system. They aren't too young for this — as long as the books have excellent illustrations and the language is clear and appropriate to the children's language level. By exposing children to the language style of non-fiction books, you are preparing them for the kinds of books they will read at school.

Before you read the book

- **Preview the book**
  Read the book beforehand to make sure it's appropriate. When you're familiar with the book's content and vocabulary, you will be better able to respond to the children's questions and comments.

- **Read the book's title, show the children the cover and encourage them to predict what the book is about**
  Encourage the children to guess what the book is about — from looking at the illustration on the cover and listening to the title. You will then be modelling the search for meaning that readers engage in before they even begin to read a book.

- **Introduce the author and illustrator**
  Tell the children who wrote and who illustrated the book and, if provided, show them the author's and illustrator's photographs. Remind them of other books written by the same author. Let them see that books are written and illustrated by ordinary people. If the children in the group have written and illustrated their own stories, let them know that they too are authors and illustrators.

- **Create a purpose for reading the book**
  Start off by creating a purpose for reading the book. For example, if you are about to read "A Promise is a Promise" by Robert Munsch, you might say "Have any of you ever made a promise, or have your parents ever made a promise to you?" After some discussion on this topic, encourage the children to find out how the promise they are going to hear about in the book is similar or different from a promise that they made or someone made to them. Such an introduction motivates the children to approach the book with a sense of purpose, encouraging them to engage in that ongoing search for meaning.

While you are reading the book

- **Take some time to respond to questions and comments**
  Children **need** to interact with both you and the book. When they point to illustrations, ask questions and make comments, they are trying to make sense of the book and relate it to what they already know (using many of the strategies you used when you read "Miranda's Miserable Day").

  Although it's not desirable to interrupt the reading of the story too often, there are ways to maintain continuity and still encourage children to be curious and interactive. Sometimes all it takes is a quick confirmation of the child's comment, such as "Yes, he **is** big isn't he?" or a brief answer to a question, such as "He doesn't want to go to sleep, that's why." Some questions need to be answered right away in order to help the child understand the story.

Sometimes you won't deal with the question or comment because the book itself will provide the answer. By saying "Let's wait and see. The book will tell us!", you can usually satisfy the child. When questions or comments are better left for discussion after you have finished reading the book, you could say "That's an interesting question. Let's talk about that at the end of the story" — and make sure that you do!

Because discussion in large groups is difficult, it's important to read books at times other than circle time, when you can interact more readily with individual children.

During these interactions, watch the quieter children. They may be initiating in their own way or they may need some encouragement to participate. A gentle comment or question may be all that's needed for a reluctant communicator to join in.

If you look closely, you'll see that each child is initiating, and you can then respond to each one.

- **Wonder aloud about what might happen next**
  Keep the search for meaning going. Saying things like, "I wonder what he'll do when he finds the treasure" shows the children you're trying to predict and will encourage them to do the same.

- **Stimulate the children to think about the story, using the "language of learning"**
  When you draw the children into a discussion about the book, encourage them to use the "language of learning" — to go beyond the book and to think about the story in many different ways.

"Fact" questions don't stimulate children to think about the story.

"Fact" questions don't stimulate children to think about the story.

Grey!

What colour is the elephant?

Grey!

Grey!

It would feel so strange to be as big and heavy as an elephant. How would you like to be this big and this heavy?

I'd like it because then I'd be the strongest animal in the world!

I wouldn't. I'd be so heavy I couldn't run fast.

I'd like it cos I could reach the leaves on the highest trees with my trunk.

This question encourages the children to use language to imagine, making them go beyond the book and think about the story in a new way.

Get the children thinking about the book by encouraging them to:

• **Predict** what will happen next

• **Draw upon their own knowledge and experiences** and relate these to the book — e.g., "Has anyone here ever been lost like the boy in this book?"

• **Project** themselves into the story and describe how they would feel or behave in that situation

• **Explain** why something happened or why one of the characters said or did something

- **Pretend/imagine** — e.g., imagine a different ending or imagine what happened beyond the ending of the story

  You can't talk about all these things at once. Favourite books should be read and reread so they turn into old friends. After repeated readings, children reach conclusions, predict, project and imagine far more easily than they can at the first reading.

- **Explain things the children don't understand**

  You need not stop every time an unfamiliar word comes up. Children learn to figure out what things mean from the context (as you did when reading "draimed" in "Miranda's Miserable Day."). However, from time to time, either children ask what a word means or you feel that an explanation is needed.

  For example, in "Each Peach Pear Plum" by Janet and Allan Ahlberg, the words "I spy" are repeated many times, and young children won't understand the word "spy." In this case, you could provide a brief explanation for the word "spy" or you could use the word in a context that makes its meaning obvious — e.g., "Who can **spy** Tom Thumb? There he is! We all **spy** Tom Thumb with our **eyes!**" As the word is repeated in this and other contexts, chances are the children will figure out its meaning before the story is over.

Explain to children what the movement lines and crumpled sheets mean.

And he couldn't sleep all night.

  To help children understand the meaning of illustrations, you can point out movement lines and facial expressions in illustrations which are unlikely to have meaning for a young child.

After reading the book

- **Encourage the children's spontaneous comments**

  Don't end the interaction as soon as you have finished reading the book. Give the children time to react to it and, to make the story more meaningful, help them relate its theme or topic to what they know and have experienced.

- **Help the children make connections between this and other books (this, too, can be done while you are reading the book)**

  Ask the children if this book reminds them of other books they have read. Draw upon what they have learned from other books and help them see the connections. You can also tell them which books this particular book reminds you of and in what way.

Ask interesting questions such as:

"Does Viola Swamp in 'Miss Nelson is Missing' in any way remind you of the wolf in 'Red Riding Hood'?" "How are they similar and how are they different?"

"Thomas in 'Thomas' Snowsuit' and Alexander in 'Where the Wild Things Are' both had trouble with adults. What kind of trouble did each one have?" "What would your Mum or Dad do if you said or did what Thomas and Alexander did?" "What would you do if you were Thomas/Alexander?"

Discussions like this help children "go beyond the book", which is what thinking readers do.

- **Offer some interesting follow-up activities**
  What about everyone getting on to all fours and pretending to be "Wild Things" after reading "Where the Wild Things are?" Or perhaps doing a fingerplay about caterpillars and butterflies after reading "The Very Hungry Caterpillar?" Or you could pretend to be dinosaurs after reading about dinosaurs, or have the children act out the story as you read it, with each child playing a small part.

  Using their bodies as well as their minds as they interact with the story brings the book to life for children and lets them imagine and interpret the book in different ways. Pretending to be a dinosaur gives the child more of an idea what it might have been like to be a fierce Tyrannosaurus Rex.

  You could also provide materials that encourage the children to create something related to the book they have read. Children might like to make a mask of ugly Viola Swamp after reading "Miss Nelson is Missing" or make thumbprint caterpillars with holes punched in them after reading "The Very Hungry Caterpillar". Or they might enjoy re-enacting a story in the puppet centre, with flannel board characters or props that they create themselves.

Pretending to be "Wild Things" brings the book "Where the Wild Things Are" to life.

- **Encourage the children to "read" the book to themselves**
  After you read a book to the children, leave it out for them, saying "The book is here if anyone would like to read it." (More than one copy of the book is desirable.) Many children will take the book and "read" it. Of course, they aren't really reading, but they are practising telling stories, using the language of books and getting a feel for reading, all of which are important in becoming a reader.

G. The Book Centre

The book centre is frequently a neglected area of the classroom. Too often, the centre faces out onto the free play area, is not enclosed, doesn't have comfortable seating and has a limited selection of books.

Most people like to read in a cosy, quiet place which has comfortable seating. Try to create such a place for the children where they can experience that same coziness; it will encourage them to go and read.

Aaaaah! This is the life!

Fill your classroom with books: big books, small books, giant books, storybooks, fun books, easy books, hard books — lots of books! Provide quality, quantity and variety.

Some suggestions for books:

— story books (including those you have read to the group)

— predictable or patterned books, which are so predictable that the children sit down and "read" them

— non-fiction books about dinosaurs, animals, insects, machines etc.

— wordless books (which encourage children to read by themselves)

— big books (those very large books, which are usually very repetitive and predictable)

— interaction books (the child has to perform some action on the book — e.g., "Pat the Bunny")

— novelty books — e.g., pop-up books

— poetry and nursery rhyme books

— children's magazines — e.g., "Sesame Street Magazine," "Big Backyard."

— teacher- or child-made books

— books made together by teachers and children

— taped books (tape yourself reading the book and provide a tape recorder with earphones)

— travel brochures

— store catalogues (especially those with toys)

— bulletin boards placed at children's eye level

H. The Writing Centre

Every preschool and kindergarten classroom needs a writing centre. Book centres encourage reading and writing centres encourage writing.

Writing and reading develop at the same time, and each one builds on the other. As children learn to read, their awareness of print helps them write, and their ability to write improves their reading. Writing centres encourage children to experiment with drawing and writing and to share what they write with others.

Set up your writing centre in a relatively quiet area, perhaps alongside the book centre, and have available a variety of writing materials that children won't be able to resist:

— chalkboard with coloured chalk

— magnetic letters

— unlined and lined paper of different colours, sizes, shapes and textures

— stapled paper books for story writing

— typewriter or computer

— cards, postcards and notepaper of various shapes and sizes

— markers, pencils, crayons, pens

— stamps and envelopes

— ink stamp, tape, stapler, glue and scissors

The materials in the writing centre should be so interesting and so varied that children see endless possibilities for their use.

Keep records of children's writing over the year. The changes in the way they write will be quite amazing.

CHAPTER 10 *Pave the Way for Young Readers and Writers* 283

I. *Make Print Talk in Your Classroom*

When children's interactions with their caregivers involve the printed word and when the use of print is demonstrated during these interactions, children become interested in print; they try to figure out what words mean and start experimenting with both reading and writing.

Child care is a wonderful place for children to learn about the printed word; it offers so many good reasons to use print and so many people to share it with. To get children interested in print, you have to show them that print, in fact, "talks". When you make print "talk", let the children see you in action so that they can watch, ask questions, make comments and see its purpose. Don't make signs and lists when the children are asleep or at home! They need to know why and how print is used and what it says.

> **Print will talk in your classroom if you provide:**
>
> - **An environment rich in the printed word (not only the alphabet but also print that has meaning)**
>
> - **Many demonstrations of how print is used**
>
> - **Interactions around the use of print**
>
> - **Opportunities for children to use and experiment with print**

Note: The following sections contain suggestions that are appropriate for use with children approximately 3 years of age and over. However, those of you who work with younger children will find that a number of the suggestions can be applied to children under age 3.

If the print in your classroom is not at the children's eye level, the children cannot benefit from it. If you want children to try to read print, don't put it where <u>you</u> can read it; put it where <u>they</u> can read it!

Use Print During Daily Routines and Activities

Adults use print as part of their everyday lives, and so should children.

- **Signs and labels**
  Use signs to communicate rules and instructions and to provide labels. Just as there are "No Parking" and "Entrance" signs in the real world, put up signs that relate to your daily routines and activities **at the children's eye level!**

  Ideas for signs:

  — Labels for cubbies, toy containers, activity centres, cupboards, supply containers

  — Signs about the number of children allowed in an activity centre; instructions for care of pets and plants

  — Signs that provide necessary information — e.g., "Fish has been fed" or "Fish has not been fed."

  — Signs that post rules which teachers have discussed and developed with the children

  — Large sheets of paper with recipes written on them — e.g., for fingerpaint or playdough — which the children watch you write

  — Signs that children make for their own purposes — e.g., "Do Not Touch" or "Keep Out"

Important information is worth reading.

- **Sign-up sheets**
  Sign-up sheets give children the opportunity to write or attempt to write their names.

  Sign-up sheets can be used to sign up for "jobs" in the classroom, for activity centres, for checking materials or books in or out, etc.

  Surveys can also be conducted, and children can sign their names to indicate their responses to the questions in the survey.

What do you like to eat on your crackers?	
Peanut butter	Cheese

- **Labelling artwork**
  Encourage children to write their names on their artwork and respond to their attempts to write their "names", even when you can't read them.

Respond to the meaning of the child's writing, even if you can't read it.

- **Attendance**
  Taking attendance can be done in a number of ways that children enjoy. When children arrive in the morning, they can:

  — put their name cards on a large chart

  — write their names on a large sheet of paper

  — check their names off a large list

  When attendance sheets are visible, children can see who is absent by looking at the list. This encourages reading.

- **Coupons**
  Let the children help you find coupons for the groceries and supplies you buy for the centre. Show them the items you need and give them supermarket flyers to page through. This is lots of fun and a good lesson in budget planning.

- **Lists**
  Lists have an important purpose in life (if you can find them when you need them), and children should be exposed to them early on. Show children how you use lists to remind you which groceries to buy or which supplies to replace. Keep your lists in visible places and let the children help you make them up, even if it means drawing the articles you need to buy. You can then write the word next to the picture.

- **Completing forms**
  Children love to imitate adults' "work". The teachers at one child care centre decided to let the children do the teacher's "job" of filling in their daily records. So they drew up a form for the children to complete when the children woke up from their nap. On this form, each child checked off whether he had a lot or a little to eat at lunch, whether he had a long or short nap, and what he did outside etc. What a wonderful, purposeful use for print.

When filling in their own daily records, children experience a real purpose for using print — and they love doing it!

Use Print for Pleasure and Social Interaction

Help children experience the pleasure that comes from using print and the opportunities it provides for social interaction.

- **Making books**

"Centre-made" books are great fun to make and read together, especially when the children are the topic of the book and when their photographs are used as illustrations. So get out your camera and take pictures of the children on a field trip, during Halloween, at the annual Christmas party or engaging in their activities on a normal day. Then, together with the children, make a book, letting them tell you what to write. Place the finished product in the book centre and watch how often they "read" their book.

Make the book together...

...and watch the children read it again and again!

Children should also be encouraged to make up their own stories. Provide blank books in the writing centre and let them know that you are available if they want to dictate a story to you. You can help them develop their story-telling skills by writing down the stories they dictate, and then reading their stories back to them. In addition to making comments on the interesting content of the story, ask scaffolding questions (see Chapter 8) to let them know which information they need to include or clarify. Make time for the children to act out the stories they write — let them assign roles and direct the "production" themselves. This is a wonderful way for them to develop their story-telling ability and to see their words transformed into a real-life play.

> *Make time for the children to act out the stories they write — let them assign roles and direct the "production" themselves. This is a wonderful way for them to develop their story-telling ability and to see their words transformed into a real-life play.*

Encourage the children to try to write their stories themselves. Reassure them that their writing doesn't have to look like an adult's and encourage them to use invented spelling, which involves spelling the word the way they hear it. Spelling, like language, develops according to a predictable sequence. In the same way that children look for grammatical patterns when learning to talk (see Chapter 7), they look for patterns in letter sequences that can be used for spelling words. We expect the child's early sentences to be short and ungrammatical, and we should expect his early attempts at spelling to be limited.

For example, look at the changes in one child's spelling of the word "train" at different ages:

HN (5 yrs, 6 mos)   HAN (5 yrs, 9 mos)   CHRAN (5 yrs, 11 mos)

TRANE (6 yrs, 3 mos)   TRAIN (6 yrs, 9 mos)

At first, children may start off writing only one letter per word (and it may not even be the right letter), but with practice and exposure, their spelling will change and develop. If children ask you how to spell a word, ask them what sounds they can hear in the word and encourage them to write these down (they tend to ignore the vowels, which is very normal). If you do spell a word for them, write it on a piece of paper while you spell it out loud. Seeing the whole word is probably easier for a young child than listening to the letters being spelled one at a time.

Encourage children to illustrate their books, and then put the books in the book centre — after all, these books are written by budding authors.

- **Rules and instructions**
Let the children see how reading is necessary for some pleasurable activities like playing a game with rules, a computer game or for assembling a toy. Let them see you read the instructions and point to the print as you read it.

- **Using Print for Dramatic play**

  Children will incorporate the use of print into their dramatic play — if you provide the necessary materials. Every dramatic play area should have pads of paper and pencils available. When the dramatic play area is a store, a bank or a post office, the children will enjoy labelling objects, writing prices on groceries, making bank deposit slips and addressing letters etc.

Dramatic and sociodramatic play are full of opportunities for reading and writing.

Use Print to Communicate with Others

It's exciting to write a letter or a card and to have someone read and appreciate it. It's also exciting to receive mail from someone else. Both of these experiences can be a regular feature of your classroom.

- **Letters and greeting cards to friends and family**

  Although you always make materials available to the children who enjoy writing letters and cards, card-making can be a special activity around Valentine's Day, Christmas Day, Mother's and Father's Day and friends' birthdays.

If you make writing materials available at all times, you may even get a birthday card yourself.

- **Letters of thanks and invitation**
  Letters of invitation to special guests or letters of thanks are also good ways of getting children involved in using print to communicate with others. Let each child contribute to a letter written on a large sheet of paper. They can either dictate their messages or write them themselves.

- **Have a mailbox in the classroom**
  Create a mailbox where children can mail their letters to you or to their friends. The mail can then be delivered to the children's labelled cubbies. Make sure that you write letters to the children at regular intervals too. Let them know that you saw how they enjoyed playing in the block centre or that you are glad they're back from vacation.

- **Penpal program**
  Consider setting up a penpal correspondence program with a neighbouring child care centre for preschoolers and kindergartners. In these programs, each child is matched with another child of the same age in the other centre, and letters are exchanged every few weeks. The children write or draw something for their penpal, put the letter in an envelope and are helped to address it. When they get their mail, a "letter carrier" is appointed to deliver the mail to the children's labelled cubbies — it's really an exciting event.

It's always exciting when the children receive letters from their penpals at a nearby child care centre — and a lot is learned about print at the same time.

This says, "This is my dog, Brandy."

- **Send letters home**
  From time to time, write personal letters to parents, telling them something that happened to their child that day — e.g., he made an interesting construction with Lego or enjoyed a new book. Discuss with the child why you are writing the letter and let him help you compose it. Make him feel important in his role as "letter carrier".

- **Badges**
  Together with the children make cardboard badges, which express the children's feelings or which send a personal message such as "I am happy that my friend Cindy is back" or "Ask me why I'm looking forward to tomorrow." Badges like these, pinned to the children's chests, are sure to get a great deal of attention from both adults and children.

Use Print to Record Information

Show children how print enables us to record and remember information. Record things on charts **at the children's eye level!**

- **Birthdays**

Put up a list of the children's names and birthdays so they can point to them and compare dates and years. You could either list them or group them according to month. You can make this chart with the children, letting them tell you their birth dates and if they can, letting them write their names. This kind of chart is useful only when it is at children's eye level.

- **Weather**

It is interesting for children in kindergarten to record weather patterns and temperature values so they can see how these change over the seasons. This also helps the development of number concepts and encourages recognition of printed words such as "snow", "sunny", "hot" and "cold". If you have cards with these words on them, the children can select the appropriate word and place it on the weather chart. This is best done informally and quickly (and not as part of every circle time) so children's interest remains high.

- **Observations**

Recordings needn't be confined to weather. You can record attendance, number of books taken from the library, favourite snacks, favourite books, number of siblings, languages spoken etc.

- **Announcements**

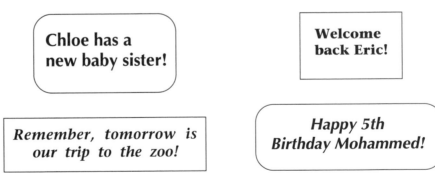

Watch children rush in and try to read your announcement, especially if their name is on it! Announcements are exciting and interesting — use them often!

- **Songs and Poems**

Happy Birthday to you,
Happy Birthday to you,
Happy Birthday dear Cindy,
Happy Birthday to you.

A well-known song encourages children to point to the words and "read" them. Introduce these charts at group or circle time and let the children read along with you. Then paste them on the wall at the children's eye level. By "reading" these charts to themselves, children begin to figure out where words begin and end, and which letters make which sounds. Soon they will start to recognize some words.

- **Open-ended bulletin boards and suggestion boards**
  Your bulletin boards can be left blank — let the children fill them in with their own artwork, letters, stories and signs.

  Have a suggestion board where children can write or draw any ideas they have for activities, outings, rules, menu items etc. And try to act on their suggestions when possible.

> *Interactive bulletin boards are a lot of fun, but they are only valuable when you talk about them with the children and when they see you write down their ideas.*

You can also create bulletin boards or charts related to a theme or to a story you have read with the children. For example, if you have read "The Very Hungry Caterpillar," you could have a bulletin board which says "The Very Hungry Children in Kindergarten: Look at what **they** ate through!" Each child could draw or write in some of the things she or he ate, and if necessary, you could write down the word underneath. Interactive bulletin boards are a lot of fun, but they are only valuable when you talk about them with the children and when they see you write down their ideas.

- **Classroom Stories**
  The children can make up a story as a group, and then dictate it to you. You write it onto a large piece of paper as they dictate, and you read aloud what you are writing as you write. For this to be effective, when the story has been written down, you should read it as a group while you point to the words, moving your finger smoothly across the lines. The children will feel as if they are reading, because they are so familiar with the story (after all, they made it up!). When this activity is over, hang the story on a board or wall, and the children will read and reread it to themselves.

Use Print to Gain Information and Knowledge

Children need a good deal of experience in using print to learn about new and interesting things.

- **Newspapers, magazines, flyers**
  Bring in newspaper articles with large, interesting pictures and read them to the children. Make sure the topic is interesting and adapt the language to the children's level.

  Make children's magazines available, as well as advertisements which might be of interest to them.

- **Maps**

  Maps are fascinating for children, especially if they identify places of personal interest, such as where the children now live and where they or others used to live.

  Place a map of the world permanently at the children's eye level and refer to it to find places mentioned in books, places where people go on vacation, places in the news, etc.

Children can discover many interesting things from reading maps.

- **Non-fiction books**

  Books are the greatest source of information, and children should often see demonstrations of books being used as a reference. Demonstrate how you use a book to gain information, showing the children the table of contents and the index.

  Books shouldn't only be placed in the book centre; they should also be placed at the science table and anywhere else where they can provide children with information. For example, teachers in a child care centre which had an earthworm composter put many books about worms near the composter and the children who were interested in the composter really enjoyed reading these books.

Summary

Child care is an ideal environment for learning about literacy because there are so many real purposes for using reading and writing. In order to help all children become readers and writers, teachers must encourage the "language of learning" during conversations and book reading and should expose children to a variety of excellent books. Book reading should be interactive, with children being encouraged to talk and think about the book in many different ways. Classrooms should have a book centre and a writing centre, and children should have many opportunities to use print as part of their daily activities, for pleasure, for communicating with others and for recording and gaining information. From participating in meaningful, purposeful print-related activities, children will begin to use reading and writing for their own purposes and will be well on their way to becoming readers and writers.

References

Ahlberg. A. & Ahlberg, J. (1978). *Each peach pear plum.* London: Penguin Books.

Allard, H. (1977). *Miss Nelson is missing.* Boston: Scholastic.

Applebee, A.N. (1978). *The child's concept of story.* Chicago: University of Chicago Press.

Booth, D., Swartz, L. & Zola, M. (1987). *Choosing children's books.* Markham, Ontario: Pembroke.

Brown, M. W. (1947). Goodnight *moon.* New York: Harper and Row.

Butler, D. (1980). *Babies need books.* New York: Atheneum.

Cambourne, B. (1988). *The whole story: Natural learning and the acquisition of literacy in the classroom.* Auckland, New Zealand: Ashton Scholastic.

Carle, E. (1987). *The very hungry caterpillar.* New York: Scholastic.

Chafel, J.A. (1982). Making early literacy a natural happening. *Childhood Education,* May/June issue, 300-304.

Church, E.B. (1991). Reading aloud to children. *Scholastic Pre-K Today,* January Issue, 38-40.

Cochrane-Smith, M. (1984). *The making of a reader.* Norwood, NJ: Ablex.

Forester, A.D. & Reinhard, M. (1989). *The learners way.* Winnipeg: Peguis .

Gillet, J.W. & Temple, C. (1986). *Understanding reading problems.* Boston: Little, Brown.

Goodman, K. & Goodman, Y. (1983). Reading and writing relationships: Pragmatic functions. *Language Arts, 60* (5), 590-599.

Goodman, K. (1986a). Reading: A psycholinguistic guessing game. *Journal of the Reading Specialist, 6,* 126-135.

Goodman, K. (1986b). *What's whole in whole language?* Richmond Hill, Ontario: Scholastic.

Goodman, Y. (1984). The development of initial literacy. In H. Goelman, A. Oberg & F. Smith, (Eds.), *Awakening to Literacy* (pp. 102-109). Exeter, NH: Heinemann.

Graves, D. & Stuart, V. (1986). *Write from the start: Tapping your child's natural writing ability.* New York: Plume.

Hill, E. (1980). *Where's Spot?* Toronto: General Publishing.

Holdaway, D. (1979). *The foundations of literacy.* Sydney, Australia: Ashton Scholastic.

Jewell, M.G. & Zintz, M.V. (1986). *Learning to read naturally.* Dubuque: Kendall Hunt.

Kimmel, M.M. & Segel, E. (1983). *For reading out loud.* New York: Delacorte Press.

Kunhardt, D. (1962). *Pat the Bunny.* Racine, Wisconsin: Western.

Lamme, L.L. (1984). *Growing up writing.* Washington, DC: Acropolis Books.

Loughlin, C.E. & Martin, M.D. (1987). *Supporting literacy: Developing effective learning environments.* New York: Teachers College Press.

Mayer, M. (1968). *There's a nightmare in my closet.* New York: Dial Books.

Mayer, M. (1975). *Just for you.* Racine, Wisconsin: Western.

Mayer, M. (1987). *Just a mess.* Racine, Wisconsin: Western .

Miller, S.A. (1991). Whole language: It's an experience! *Scholastic Pre-K Today,* January Issue, 44-72.

Munsch, R. (1985). *Thomas' snowsuit.* Toronto: Annick Press.

Munsch, R. (1987). *I have to go.* Toronto: Annick Press.

Munsch, R. (1988). *A promise is a promise.* Toronto: Annick Press.

Perkins, A. (1969). *Hand, hand, fingers, thumb.* New York: Random House.

Sendak, M. (1983). *Where the wild things are.* New York: Scholastic.

Strickland, D. & Morrow, L.M. (Eds). (1989). *Emerging literacy: Young children learning to read and write.* Newark, DE: International Reading Association.

Taylor, D. (1983). *Family literacy: Young children learning to read and write.* Exeter, NH: Heinemann.

Teale, W.H. & Sulzby, E. (Eds.), (1985). *Emergent literacy: Writing and reading.* Norwood, NJ: Ablex .

Temple, C.A., Nathan, R.G. & Burris, N.A. (1982). *The beginnings of writing.* Boston, Mass: Allyn and Bacon.

van Kleeck, A. (1982). *Metalinguistics and language disorders in children: Does meta matter?* Miniseminar presented at the American Speech-Language Hearing Association Annual Convention, Toronto, Canada.

van Kleeck, A. (1990). Emergent Literacy: Learning about print before learning to read. *Topics in Language Disorders, 10* (2), 24-45.

CHAPTER 11

Circle Time: An Interactive Language-Learning Experience

A. Circle Time — Time to Have Fun and Learn Language

We know that children learn language naturally during their day-to-day interactions with their caregivers. So what does a formal, structured activity like circle time (also known as group time) contribute to language learning and literacy?

Some teachers say "Children learn to listen at circle time." But others disagree, saying that children listen better in small, informal groups.

Some teachers say "Circle time encourages children to share ideas and experiences." But others disagree, saying that a lot more sharing takes place at the lunch table and in small, informal groups.

Some teachers say "You can teach concepts at circle time." Again, many others disagree, saying that the most learning takes place when children are involved in hands-on activities with an interested teacher nearby.

However, many teachers believe that circle time is valuable and are seeking ways to make it an experience as rich and stimulating as possible.

When children aren't interested in the topic and when circle time goes on for too long, its purpose is lost — and so is the children's attention.

Let's begin with the assumption that the purpose of circle time is for the children to have fun and to learn. If activities at circle time are planned with this purpose in mind, then children can:

- expand their ability to use the language of learning

- expand their understanding and knowledge of familiar topics

- expand their general knowledge to include unknown topics

- be encouraged to use their imaginations

- learn to share information with a group of children

- expand their story-telling abilities

The suggestions that follow are most appropriate for children who are 3 years of age and older.

B. Set the Stage for Successful Circle Time

Circle time involves a lot more than getting the children together in a group. When you give some thought to the set-up and organization of circle time, you set the stage for success.

Small Groups are Best

Small groups allow for more interaction, participation and individual attention. Teachers who are able to stagger circle time or who have two small groups, each with one teacher, find this situation preferable.

Choose an Appropriate Time and Place

The best time to have circle is before the children get tired, restless and hungry. In many classrooms, circle time is early in the morning, before free play.

Children feel more comfortable during circle time if they are in a cosy corner on a soft rug or mat, and they will be less distractable if there are no toys or equipment nearby to tempt them.

Start Something Interesting Before All the Children have Gathered

Rather than waiting for everyone to join the group and getting annoyed with children who are taking too long, begin with an upbeat song or fingerplay. Or, as one imaginative teacher suggested, create a make-believe spaceship and invite children to walk along a make-believe ramp, up some "stairs" and into your spaceship, which is about to leave for an exciting place. In this way, the children who are already sitting in the group get involved quickly and the others hurry to join them because they don't want to miss out.

Be an Entertaining Entertainer

This is one time when you need to be a good entertainer! Whether you are telling a story, explaining a game, describing something, introducing a theme or singing a song, your style sets the tone for the group. Your animation and enthusiasm will rub off on the children and will be reflected in their interest and involvement.

Be Prepared to Change Your Plans

Things don't always go according to plan. The children may not be interested in the topic you have chosen, or they may be interested in a different aspect of it. They might want to continue with one activity longer than you had planned or have you repeat it. Be flexible and willing to adapt or change your plans — that's the way to encourage children's curiosity and keep them interested.

Short and Sweet is Best

The principle in this case is "Quit while you're ahead." Don't drag out circle time, even if one or two children are still attending. Cater to the majority — and that usually means stopping while everyone is still attending, involved and stimulated.

Use Large, Appealing Props

Props attract children's attention and provide additional visual cues. They should be large, clear, appealing and appropriate. If they aren't, the children lose their focus as they push others aside to try to see them.

C. The 6 Is: A Guide for Planning and Conducting Circle Time

The 6 Is provide you with practical guidelines for planning and conducting circles which expand children's language, general knowledge, imagination, ability to share information with a group and story-telling.

A circle or group time should be:

- **Interesting**
- **Informative**
- **Introduced**
- **Interrelated (with other topics and activities)**
- **Interactive**
- **Imaginative**

Putting the 6 Is into Practice

1. The topic and activities must be INTERESTING to the children

Choose a theme or topic that is appropriate to the children's ages and interests. If the topic of your circle is related to the theme of the week (or month), make sure that your theme is drawn from the children's interests. Last year's group may have been fascinated by bugs, but this year's may be interested in dinosaurs, outer space or sea creatures. It's seldom a good idea to repeat the same themes year after year!

When children are interested in the topic, they do more than listen. They search for meaning by analyzing what they hear and drawing conclusions about it. They relate what they hear to what they already know, predict what will happen next and use their imaginations to visualize what you are talking about. In other words, they use the language of learning as they build their general knowledge and understanding of the world around them.

2. The topic should be INFORMATIVE

Too often, themes are chosen in order to teach concepts like colours, shapes or farm animals. Not only are such topics uninformative (most preschoolers already know them) but they are also extremely concrete. Because children as young as 3 years have vivid imaginations and are very curious, your themes should encourage them to go beyond concrete concepts such as colours and shapes.

You don't need to abandon familiar topics, however; topics such as colours and pets can provide a base for expanding children's knowledge.

> *Because children as young as 3 years have vivid imaginations and are very curious, your themes should encourage them to go beyond concrete concepts such as colours and shapes.*

edge. For example, while names of colours are familiar to most preschoolers and kindergartners, the colour wheel and primary and secondary colours are not. If children are taught about primary and secondary colours and are given opportunities to mix powder paint to make new colours, they can learn a great deal. A theme about pets could also go beyond names and descriptions of pets and could include their eating habits, physical characteristics, ancestors, locomotion etc.

New topics are fascinating to children, especially at the kindergarten stage — and when you research these topics, you may discover some fascinating new facts yourself! One teacher who was doing research on the theme "Dangerous Sea Creatures" was surprised to discover that most sharks are not man-eaters and that the whale shark, the largest shark of all, has allowed divers to ride on its back!

Be cautious about focusing on festivals or holiday themes such as Easter or Halloween weeks in advance of the event. Although painting eggs and dressing up for Halloween are fun for children, these topics have no meaning for those children who don't understand the idea of an annual event and who don't remember it from the previous year. 3-year-olds don't know what the significance of a pumpkin is when it's introduced early in October. But if you introduce the theme just before Halloween and then explore it in more detail **after** Halloween (when the children's experience of Halloween is recent and meaningful), they will be ripe to learn more about it.

3. The topic needs to be INTRODUCED

Always introduce the topic to the group; this orients the children and stimulates them to draw upon their background knowledge in order to make sense of what will be discussed.

You need to reintroduce the topic each day that you discuss it. Children don't automatically know that today's discussion or story is related to yesterday's. Your introduction helps them make this connection.

4. The topic or theme should be INTERRELATED with other topics and activities throughout the day

Children learn new concepts when these build upon what they already know and are presented as part of an integrated whole (not as an isolated piece of information). That's why teaching through themes helps children learn.

Circle time provides you with opportunities to introduce a new theme or topic, to interrelate new with old knowledge and to reinforce and expand on it. As children gain new knowledge, they reorganize their view of the world and develop a more integrated understanding of it. The more knowledge they have, the more background knowledge they bring with them to the books they read and the stories they write.

To help children interrelate and integrate their new knowledge, themes should be incorporated into a number of learning experiences throughout the day. There should be many opportunities for hands-on activities, for exploring materials and resources on the topic, for discussion, observation and for theme-related dramatic play.

> *To make learning meaningful, new knowledge should always be interrelated with old knowledge.*

For example, if your theme is "Water", children could be provided with opportunities to do some of the following:

— play with water, snow and ice and compare their properties

— experiment with what dissolves and what doesn't dissolve in water

— experiment with objects that sink and float

— make paper boats and sail them at the water table

— read books about water

— look at a globe to see how much of the Earth consists of water

— paint with different coloured water

— play with bubbles in water

— make books about water

— play in the dramatic play area, which has been transformed into a ship or a beach

Notice that none of these activities involves following teacher's directions or copying a teacher's model. Drawing or pasting onto teacher's "cut-outs" doesn't provide children with opportunities to explore, experiment and discover. Theme-related activities should always be relatively open-ended and should allow for individual children to explore and discover in their own way.

5. Circle time should be INTERACTIVE

Although circle time is carefully planned and directed by you, the children should play an active role in it. Sitting quietly and listening does not guarantee learning. The more actively involved the children are, the more learning there will be. Of course, there will be times when you will talk and they will listen, but those times should be followed by interactive group activities.

- **Plan for a change of pace**
  Pacing of activities is critical in circle time. Plan for energetic activities to follow listening times, for child talk to follow teacher talk, for something novel to follow something familiar. Keep the children involved and participating at different levels and in different ways!

  There are many ways to make circle time more active and interactive:

  — group discussions

  — group games (especially cooperative games)

  — storytelling (to which the children contribute)

  — fingerplays

  — action songs

  — drama (acting out something related to the theme or topic)

  — creating experience charts

  — group read-alouds from a story or chart

  — children creating, drawing or writing something in response to a story or theme and sharing it with the group

Every child enjoys this kind of energetic activity, especially after sitting still for a while.

Hands-on experience with a parachute gets the children actively involved in the theme of "Air Transportation."

- **Encourage interaction through sharing ideas and information**

  At circle time, many teachers give children opportunities to share information with the group. For example, children may describe an experience or provide information on an object they have brought for Show and Tell. This kind of "sharing" is different from an exchange of information during informal conversation because it involves addressing a group and presenting information in a clear, organized way (similar to the type of language required for telling good stories).

  "Sharing" at circle time can be a valuable experience for children, but it can also be boring. If every child is given a turn at one sitting or if the teacher ends up doing all the talking and asking question after question, sharing is no fun at all.

- **"Sharing" at circle time can work if:**
  — not every child "shares" at each circle, but gets a turn during the week

  — children do as much of the talking as possible

  — children are encouraged to share experiences and ideas and not just show off toys

  — children are given the opportunity to hold their own sharing times in small groups, with one child being the "leader" and fielding questions and comments from the other children. With some support and specific guidelines, children at the kindergarten level are mature enough to conduct sharing time alone. With practice, it can work.

- **Scan to keep track of children's attention and interest**

  At circle time, when you keep track of the children's involvement and interest (which is demonstrated by their attention and participation), you gain important information about what each child needs from you. In order to provide each child with the attention and encouragement she needs during circle time, you must be aware of her level of involvement.

  During circle time, scan the group to see where each child falls on this continuum:

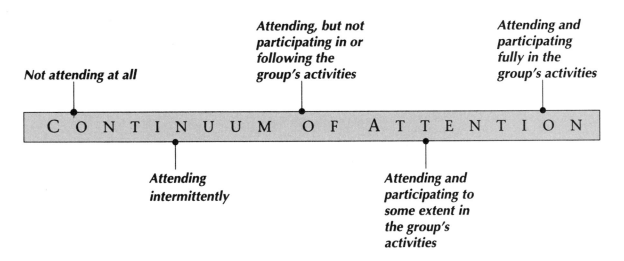

  — *Children who are not attending at all*

  If most of the group aren't attending, perhaps the topic is inappropriate or there's too much sitting and listening. In this case, the children need activities that are more active and interactive.

  If only one or two children aren't attending, they may be uninterested or unable to follow the topic. If they are unable to follow the topic, another teacher may need to sit with them and explain what is being discussed.

  Children who frequently disrupt circle time may be telling you in their own way that they can't understand the discussion and that they haven't developed the ability to attend for very long. Making circles more active and interactive helps these children stay involved. However, if they still disrupt the group, consider allowing them to play quietly somewhere else. In time, as they mature and develop more advanced language skills, they should be able to attend and participate.

Sometimes, children don't attend because they are too far away from you. Moving them in across from you (not next to you, where they can't see you, the book or prop) may get them more involved. Calling them by name to make them feel included may also help focus them on the activity.

— *Children who are attending intermittently*
When children attend intermittently, you can often draw them back into the activity by moving them closer, calling them by name or saying something personal such as, "You've been to a beach like this one, haven't you, Matthew?"

— *Children who are attending, but who are not participating in or following the group's activities*
You have the child's attention, but perhaps she's reluctant or too shy to join in. Seat the child in the front and centre of the group so you can make easy eye contact with her.

Children like this need time to get comfortable, as well as to receive a smile of encouragement. When they take the risk of joining in, it may be better not to make too much of a fuss — their reward comes from the pleasure of involvement, not from praise.

— *Children who are attending and participating to some extent in the group's activities*
Perhaps these children don't fully understand what's required of them, although they really want to join in. Make sure that you clarify what the activity or topic is about. Often children who speak English as a second language don't have the receptive language skills to participate fully. When their receptive language skills improve, they are likely to participate more actively.

— *Children who are attending and participating fully in the group's activities*
These children may be getting all your attention — watch out!

6. Circle time should include activities which are IMAGINATIVE

The ability to pretend and imagine plays an important role in children's understanding and appreciation of stories and in the development of literacy (see Chapter 10). Circle time is a prime opportunity to get children involved in using language to create make-believe and to engage in dramatizations.

Using drama in a group, where everyone pretends without realistic props, is fun and helps children develop the ability to use make-believe. For example, you can model the use of language to create make-believe by telling the children that a parachute is going to become a huge popcorn maker. When they hold the parachute and shake it up and down, they pretend to make popcorn and then pretend to eat it once all the popcorn has "popped".

We're going to imagine that we've all taken parachuting lessons and that we're all experienced parachutists. We're going to pretend to go up into the air in a plane and when we're flying high above the clouds we're all going to jump out of the plane and parachute down to the ground!

Language can bring exciting imaginary experiences to life!

Jumping out of an imaginary plane with an imaginary parachute is really exciting!

Remember to open your parachutes after you jump!

Here I go!

HAPPY HOLIDAYS AIRLINES

Circle time is the perfect time for thematic fantasy play (based on a story or rhyme) which encourages the use of language to create make-believe. After reading a story, give everyone a role to play and let the children act out the story. Not only is this a lot of fun but it helps children understand the story better. It also develops their **sense** of story, which is important for understanding stories in books.

Thematic fantasy play develops children's imagination and makes stories come alive.

Summary

When circle time is interesting, informative and interactive, teachers promote the kind of language use that enables children to become successful readers and writers. Instead of sitting and listening, children become actively involved in group activities such as drama, story-telling, action songs and group games, activities which build upon their background knowledge, expand their general knowledge and encourage them to use their imaginations. To help every child participate, teachers must scan the group to monitor each child's attention and involvement. When necessary, they can provide extra encouragement and attention to children who are not fully involved in the group's activities.

References

Bredenkamp, S (Ed.). (1987). *NAEYC position statement on developmentally appropriate practice in programs for 4-and 5-year-olds.* Washington,DC: National Association for the Education of Young Children.

Hendrick, J. (1990). Total learning: D*evelopmental curriculum for the young child.* Columbus, OH: Merrill.

McCracken, R.A. & McCracken, M.J. (1987). *Reading is only the tiger's tail: A language arts program.* Winnipeg, Canada: Peguis.

Moyer, J., Egertson, H. & Isenberg, J. (1987). The child-centred kindergarten. *Childhood Education, 63*(4), 235-242.

Nash, C. (1989). *The learning environment: A practical approach to the education of the three-, four- and five-year old.* Don Mills: Collier McMillan Canada.

Siks, G.B. (1983). *Creative drama with children.* New York: Harper and Row.

Wilmes, L. & Wilmes, D. (1983). *Everyday circle times.* Elgin, IL: Building Blocks.

Detailed Table of Contents

CHAPTER 2

The Stages of Language Development: Talking Takes Time 43

PART 4

LET LANGUAGE LEAD THE WAY TO LITERACY   254

CHAPTER 11

Circle Time: An Interactive Language-Learning Experience 299